GREATNESS GUIDE

A Coaching Manual for Sales Professionals in the Low Voltage Systems Industry

Andy Bernot

In memory of Jack "Jackie" Howard,

Great friend and fierce competitor who

Achieved Personal Greatness

Acknowledgements

Over the past 40 years I have had the great honor to work with and learn from many excellent sales professionals and sales leaders. The selfless sharing of their knowledge and their philosophies has made a lasting impression and shaped my perceptions of success within our industry. The list of influencers is too extensive to identify here but I trust my fellow colleagues will recognize the moments where we shared a learning or some profound revelation.

Many thanks to my close friends that offered input on early drafts of this book. Special thanks to Frank Cappello and my wife Cindy for their massive contributions in editing, challenging content and offering refinements.

Contents

Introduction

This manual has been developed to guide you in your quest to achieve personal greatness. The information contained within has been shared with many before you and has been proven beneficial. All sales professionals have access to much of the same information, although few use it to their competitive advantage. The variability of sales success follows the normal distribution curve (bell curve). This guide is designed to move you to the extreme left end of the normal distribution curve (the success side), to make you an outlier as a peak performer. Increasing your probability of success requires that we agree on a model as to how individuals learn, grow and transform their lives.

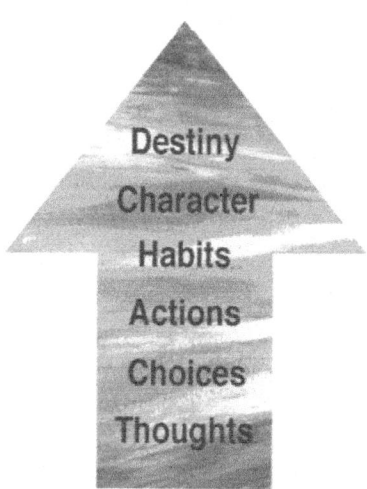

This guide intends to affect your thinking about the many aspects of the low voltage systems business in order to generate useful **Thoughts** that have proven successful by industry peers. With those thoughts you will make **Choices,** internalize information and determine what you will accept. **Action** is the next critical step, and clearly, knowledge without action results in nothing. Your purposeful actions will determine your success.

As you see the positive effects of your actions you will repeat them thereby developing the **Habits** that will improve your efficiency and effectiveness. Your belief and discipline to your habits will develop your personal leadership qualities that define your **Character.** Good thoughts, good choices, good actions and good habits strengthen your character and lead you to your **Destiny** of personal greatness.

What is personal greatness?

Personal greatness is realizing your full potential as a sales professional and as a human. Realizing your full potential is simple in concept, but it is not easy. I believe the strategy of achieving personal greatness can be defined in four aspects: effort, principles, growth and service.

Max Effort: Others may motivate you, but you are the only one who knows if you have applied maximum effort. Most people, when being objective, acknowledge that maximum effort is rarely applied. Your absolute best efforts are a key element in achieving personal greatness.

Hero Principles: What is your image of Hero Principles? Think about the people you personally hold in highest regard as well as history's great leaders. Hero Principles include integrity, courage, accountability, humility, compassion and generosity. You decide which principles resonate most with you. The second element of achieving personal greatness is consistently living Hero Principles every day.

Personal Growth: The expression "What got you here, won't get you there" is appropriate when discussing the prospect of achieving personal greatness. Regardless of your current skill set, you can and must get better. Although personal growth happens naturally from day to day experiences, individuals who aspire to achieve personal greatness realize the need to be intentional about their personal growth. They have a plan and they set goals for themselves that makes them more valuable.

7

Serve Others: The final element in achieving personal greatness is the passion and excellence in which you serve others. The list of others includes clients, peers, supervisors, and community stakeholders. When applying your maximum effort with noble principles for the benefit of others you are demonstrating personal leadership. As you intentionally learn and grow you expand your excellence in serving the world and consequently move closer to achieving your full potential.

Personal greatness awaits you. Section 1 of this Greatness Guide will help prepare you for your journey.

Section 1 - Preparing for Your Journey

Sales as a Career

Why does somebody choose sales as a career? The motivations for embarking on a sales career may be a desire to apply a business degree earned in college, a necessary stepping-stone to gain a management position, the desire to earn big commissions or a job that allows for independence and freedom. These are common motivators among most sales colleagues. Selling is highly competitive and for individuals who love the thrill of winning, selling can duplicate those great feelings. Additionally, selling is about serving. Serving your clients better than they have ever been served. To serve others well is not common, it takes integrity, empathy, intelligence, critical thinking and communications.

Consider these questions:

- Why do I want to be a sales professional?
- Why do I want to be in this industry and this company?
- What is my personal vision and mission?

Many individuals entering the sales profession can articulate why they want to be a sales professional. However, most do not know why they want to be in the life safety/security/low voltage industry. Few sales professionals have formulated a personal vision and mission.

We arrive at life's opportunity points from different directions and with different perspectives. Since you are here with us now, we are vested in your personal growth and development. Achieving greatness as a sales professional is no easy task and there are no shortcuts to success. You must progress daily. Your probability of success will be greatly enhanced by remaining intentional with your growth and development.

You possess a healthy desire to achieve success! Your life is precious and under your control. You choose to honor it by defining your mission and applying focus and energy to the achievement of personal greatness.

Your Role

As a sales professional you play an essential role in growing the business and supporting operations.

Growing Business:

When I refer to growth, I am describing the growth of bookings, backlog, revenues, and gross margins. To achieve those outcomes, you will need to develop a business plan. When building your plan, you may consider the strategies deployed by successful senior sales colleagues or develop your own unique course. Ultimately, there is both a high degree of autonomy and accountability within this role.

Brand Manager:

You are the face of the organization. In your role you communicate the organization's capabilities and values. With your communication skills you convey the brand of the organization. You provide consulting services to your clients. It is imperative that you strive for Win/Win agreements between the client and the company. You are expected to be both advocate for our customers and to act as owner of your position on the team, which includes looking out for the interests of the company.

Team Member:

The business process involves many functional resources to deliver successful projects and services. Those resources have specific roles and goals. To deliver great project and service results requires having great personnel, great processes and great leadership. As a team member you are expected to be one of those great personnel who follows and performs great processes and who takes on a leadership role.

Your leadership role is not one of positional power, rather it is a leadership based on influence. This is demonstrated through excellence of actions, skills and traits. A short list of examples includes:

- Providing high quality proposals that have been coordinated with operations and service.

- Enthusiasm in turnover meetings and kickoff meetings.

- Encouraging and motivating team members to achieve excellence.

- Remaining involved and supportive throughout the life of the project.

- Demonstrating integrity in all matters.

You serve a critical role within the organization as do every one of your teammates. With your effective leadership you will facilitate teamwork, harmony, creativity and commitment that will result in phenomenal project outcomes and delighted customers.

Vision

You have taken on an important role within a dynamic organization. The terms <u>roles, goals and responsibilities</u> are common among all positions. Every team member has a responsibility to deliver on a result. Those results may be quantitative, as in selling a certain volume of work at a prescribed margin. The results may also be qualitative, as in following and performing to established process requirements. The key point here is that these roles, goals and responsibilities have been assigned to you and are a minimum requirement to keep the machine running. You are a vital cog in the organizational machine, but it is beneficial to understand the bigger picture, the vision of the organization.

Vision, in this context, is the practice of seeing beyond the present reality. To create in the mind what does not currently exist in order to become something better in the future.

The vision of the world's best organizations has something in common, they understand where they are going, how they are going to get there and what their Utopia will look like once they arrive. Research has shown that companies that have a clear vision perform better in the marketplace. This is understood to be true, for when a group of people have a shared vision of what they are building and believe strongly in the mission they are inspired, and they can see how their efforts contribute to the vision.

The company's vision has been condensed to a <u>vision statement</u> which is useful to leadership, colleagues and clients:

- **For leadership,** the vision statement challenges the on-going evaluation of the markets being served and the products and services offered. The vision statement also guides the evaluation of financial investments and strategies to achieve growth.

- **For colleagues**, the vision statement provides clarity of where the organization is going and inspires them to want to make meaningful contributions over the long haul.
- **For clients**, the vision statement will help them determine if the cultures are compatible. Do philosophies align?

It is also true to say that not all colleagues are inspired by a vision statement. This can be attributed to the way individuals interpret the Why behind the vision. As an example, the vision necessarily describes what is being built which is often referred to in dollars of growth over a period of years. Understandably, this metric on the surface does not create excitement but with little imagination it becomes clear that financial growth is the catalyst for colleagues to grow into new positions, gain promotions and have challenging work.

As a final point, consider how creating a personal vision statement would benefit you. Think of your personal assignment:

- What are you building?
- What markets are you serving?
- What products and services are you providing?
- Who are your target customers?
- How big will your personal business be in five years?

The organization's vision is to achieve greatness. It can only achieve this vision through colleagues with a passion to achieve both personal and team greatness. I advise you to DREAM BIG.

Mission

When I was a rookie sales representative, I was committed to give maximum effort every day. I had a positive attitude, I cared about other people and I possessed a keen sense of curiosity to learn as much as possible as quickly as possible. I had success in achieving my sales goals and made steady progress for the next two years. I was driven to achieve goals and to live up to expectations of my manager and customers.

Then came the proverbial <u>Ah Ha</u> moment. I had discovered an audio recording of the *One-Minute Sales Person* by Spencer Johnson[1]. This was my introduction to the concept of mission. The presentation of the information was logical and compelling. It required me to think about why my business exists, who I serve and what I do for them. The lesson also introduced the power of having a mission statement and gave the example as follows:

> *"My mission as sales representative for the ABC Company is to provide my customers with the <u>good feelings</u> they want from the products and services I have to offer."*

I suspect that the reader of this mission statement may question why this rather simple statement became a catalyst for me. What hit me then and has been confirmed many times over the next 35 years was the power of having a clear understanding of my purpose in business and by extension my purpose in life.

At that point in time, I realized alignment. Now combining effort, enthusiasm, proper principles and a clear mission I discovered a greater energy and power that made me feel unstoppable.

Since then, I have coached many sales professionals and leaders in the development of their mission and mission statement. Some have

---

[1] Kenneth Blanchard, Ph.D., Spencer Johnson, M.D., *The One-Minute Sales Person*

had similar experiences to mine, but sadly, many have not. The explanation for this may be captured in the expression "No wine before its time" meaning that a person must sense the benefit of wrestling with the heady question of "What is my mission?" Furthermore, they believe that clarity of mission will guide them to achieve personal greatness.

I encourage you to research mission statements and to think deeply about your mission. In addition to *The One-Minute Sales Person* you can gain great insight from *7 Habits of Highly Effective People*. There are no parameters to writing a mission statement, but experience shows that the best mission statements are short, memorable and have an emotional element. Determining and committing to the achievement of your mission will propel you on your journey to achieve personal greatness.

Attitude

Trying to describe one's attitude is a very broad exercise. We are all a product of our personal history and understandably we all view the world from our own unique perspective. The fact that our attitudes are unique makes for a very interesting world when we interact with others.

So how does the discussion of attitude fit into your journey to achieve personal greatness? It has to do with self-awareness. How do you view yourself as a person? As a citizen? As a sales professional? How would you describe your world view in each of these roles?

There is no shortage of books that can detail what many successful people believe to be their secret to achieving results. Their attitudes and philosophies are provided for our consideration, as they believe their attitude was their differentiator. Not surprisingly, many of the core beliefs are shared by industry superstars.

Let's explore some of the noteworthy **characteristics of the best sales professionals** who have achieved greatness in our industry.

- **Positivity:** They are resilient and have grit. They understand that perception is reality, so they approach all interactions with intentionality. They are grounded in the reality that selling is a complex business and things do not always go as planned or desired. They have the maturity and discipline to control their emotions and inspire others.

- **Effort:** They understand that sales is a combination of art and math. The math proves that more repetitions leads to improved competence and competence leads to results. The greatest performers understand that they must make sacrifices to be a champion. They invest more time and work harder than most.

- **Empathy:** They care about others. They understand that the best agreements are Win/Win.

- **Ego:** They are competitive, and they desire to be the Best of the Best. Harvard Business Review[2] conducted a study on the attributes of the best salespersons and found they ranked high in both empathy and ego; they desired to be the best in the world in taking care of their clients' needs.

- **Proactive:** They are predisposed to taking action. Steven Covey's book, *7 Habits of Highly Effective People*, describes proactivity as working on things that are Important but not yet Urgent.[3]

- **Continuous Improvement:** They are consciously competent in their profession as a sales executive. They are committed to a lifetime of learning and growing both personally and professionally and they strive to realize their full potential.

- **Responsibility:** They adopt the mantra of "If it is to be, it is up to me!"

You would be well served to consider these attitudinal characteristics in your personal philosophy as they have been proven in the careers of the Best of the Best.

---

[2] David Mayer, Herbert Greenberg, *Harvard Business Review July-August 2006, What Makes a Good Salesman*
[3] Steven R. Covey, *The 7 Habits of Highly Effective People*, pp.73-101 *(Simon & Schuster, New York, 2004)*

Mantra

Many people have a key word or phrase that they recite to themselves that motivates them to act or align themselves with their core beliefs. Mantras are powerful. They are a mental tool that can be likened to flipping an electrical switch to energize an appliance.

Steve Zehner was the senior sales representative when I started my sales career. He shared his mantra with me which was "WWB is the key; Working, Wanting, Believing." The thing I remember about my early discussions with Steve was his absolute conviction to this philosophy and his congruency of action.

- *Working* was his word for giving effort, for putting in the repetitions, for the extra sales call, for discipline and excellence. You could feel the linkage to Vince Lombardi and a pride that came with giving maximum effort every day.
- *Wanting* was his word for desire. The desire to achieve goals, the desire to serve the customer, the desire to achieve excellence and the desire to be the absolute best he could be. Steve wanted to achieve personal greatness.
- *Believing* was his word for confidence and faith. It was his belief that by putting in the work and achieving his goals with excellence that all good things would follow. No obstacle was too big, nothing could stop his inevitable victory.

What is your mantra? What is the word or phrase that prepares you for the battles of the day? When they write your life story your mantra will be the title of the book. Make it compelling.

Integrity

Many organizations establish a code of standards, key principles or core values for the purpose of defining the culture they are promoting or are aspiring to create. These efforts attempt to distill the many important principles of life into the critical few that are viewed as most important to the organization at a point in time. Not surprisingly, the core value of <u>integrity</u> continues to be on the list of most organizations. It seems evident that integrity is vital in every aspect of our lives and thus worthy to promote with rigor.

How do we measure integrity? Are there degrees of integrity or is it simply a yes/no answer? When we look at others can we determine integrity by their actions? When we evaluate organizations, do we judge their integrity by the actions of their members? Can individuals and organizations who have had lapses in integrity rebound in the opinions of the world? These questions lead us to understand that we are not perfect as individuals nor as organizations.

You cannot achieve personal greatness without the consistent pursuit of living a life of integrity. This pursuit includes all dimensions of your life; business, family and community. Lack of integrity in one area will affect your life balance. As you practice integrity and consciously recognize your congruency, you become stronger and build your resolve to always be true to yourself and your commitment to integrity.

Only you know if you are acting with integrity. Others will develop an opinion about you and your integrity based on your words and actions, but over time the truth will become evident. I recall hearing an interview where the speaker made a claim that shaped my awareness of world perception's. The statement was "We measure others by their <u>actions</u>, we measure ourselves by our <u>intentions.</u>" How does your intentions toward integrity compare with your actions? Thoughts matter, words matter, actions matter.

Here are some of the practical reminders of integrity within your role as a sales professional:

- Make and keep commitments.
- Always be honest in communications with transparency of your agenda.
- Always think and deal in the best interests of the customer over your personal gain.
- Treat everyone you meet as the most important person in the world (because that person believes that they are).
- Do not say anything about others in their absence that you would not say if they were present.

Integrity is the central component of your personal leadership. It is essential to handle life's most difficult challenges. Your integrity will be the catalyst for achieving greatness both personally and for your organization.

Section 2 – Professional Behaviors

Every Day is Game Day

As the sales professional you are the front liner to your customers. Comparing your business to a sporting event, you are the key player in the game. You must be prepared to **GO** every day.

Your success will be determined by your customers. If they see greater value in your products and services over those of your competitors, you will be rewarded. For customers to determine the value of your products and services they need to understand their features, functions and benefits. You perform the essential role in communicating and educating the customers on your value proposition.

Winning the confidence of a customer has many variables, some of those variables are within your control and others are not. The variables that you control include:

- **Dress attire:** Research the culture of the customer, understand what they prefer as a dress code for their colleagues and potential business partners. It may require you to dress a notch above or below your internal standards. Wearing a three-piece suit to a central Texas oil field would be ill advised as would be wearing casual attire to most law firms.
- **Be prepared:** Have a written call plan with clearly stated objectives.
- **Research your client:** Understand their business and their core values. Synthesize how that information aligns with your mission, vision and values.
- **Articulation**: Your ability to deliver a clear and logical communication will build positive perception.
- **Problem diagnosis:** Your skill in describing the client's problem will establish your credibility.
- **Proposing solutions**: Presenting reasonable and innovative solutions to the client's problems builds confidence.

24

A champion comes to the game prepared to win. They visualize successful outcomes; they are confident and poised to accept the challenge of the day. The champion will not waste the opportunity to win today's game.

The best teams have leaders that set the tone. Leaders build and support a culture of excellence which is achieved through preparation, persistence, professionalism and positive energy. They have an attitude of <u>win today</u>.

Every day is <u>Game Day</u>. Sales professionals strive to maximize time in front of customers. They enjoy the art of selling and serving clients, the more the better. Office days are not relaxation days. Sales professionals know that when opportunity knocks, they will be prepared.

Office Behavior

Three questions:

- Have you ever thought about how your actions influence the culture of an organization?
- Have you ever thought about how the culture of an organization affects your behavior?
- Which companies come to mind when you think of great cultures?

The shaping of an organizations culture is evolving all the time. Culture can be shaped voluntarily or involuntarily. Every action you make has an impact in shaping culture. Many actions seem inconsequential; however, they all have a cause and effect to other actions. Multiply this by millions of actions by the entire work force and the result is cultural evolution.

You have real power to promote a positive culture. So, what promotes a positive culture:

- **Attitude:** "I am a leader". Behave as if the future of the world is your responsibility (it is).
- **Energy:** Be focused, determined and enthusiastic.
- **Beauty:** Keep work areas organized and tidy.
- **Humanity:** Be respectful of all people.
- **Safety:** Be aware of safety and take actions to protect yourself and others.
- **Civility:** Use professional language and avoid offensive language.
- **Respect:** Be sensitive and respectful to the work areas of others.
- **Caring:** Be aware of the needs of others.
- **Helpfulness:** Lend a helping hand to others.

Your behaviors define you. There is an expression "What you are speaks so loudly that I can't hear a word you say." Recognize that your behaviors have a significant impact on the future of the organization. Your positive behaviors will be appreciated by your fellow colleagues who will respond in kind and follow your lead. The positive actions of many will ensure that the organizations culture is energizing. An energizing culture is a force multiplier for you to achieve personal greatness.

Communication Etiquette

As a sales professional you are looked upon as a professional communicator. When one is considered a _professional_ the expectations of performance are elevated. Every professional recognizes the need to practice the basics to remain sharp because, even professionals can get sloppy in their performance.

Communication etiquette is primarily about respect. Some of the notable areas of respect include:

- Respecting the dignity of others
- Respecting people's time
- Respecting the safety of others
- Respecting other's opinions
- Respecting the property of others

Most communication interactions, whether in office, on-line, phone or in social settings, will fit into one of these categories. Some examples of positive and negative behaviors include:

Behavior	Positive	Negative
Respecting the dignity of others	• Engaging and positive language • Providing constructive information • Recognition and affirmation of contributions	• Using unprofessional language • Gossiping • Passive aggressive behavior

Behavior	Positive	Negative
Respecting other people's time	• Being on time for meetings • Confirming meeting time duration • Concluding meetings at scheduled time	• Interrupting the work of others • Rambling conversations unrelated to business issue • Sending poor business communications
Respecting the safety of others	• Respect others physical space • Being a good steward to the environment • Use positive and affirming language	• Using spiteful and angry communication • Careless comments on social media • Inappropriate use of humor
Respecting other's opinions	• Active listening to others • Seeking to understand • Offering balanced feedback	• Emotional responses • Sarcastic responses • Ignoring requests
Respecting the property of others	• Efficient use of resources • Keeping spaces organized and tidy • Cleaning or repairing your creations	• Plagiarizing the work of others • Criticizing the work of others • Defaming the reputation of others

Everything you say and do reflects your communication etiquette. It is important that you are aware of your behaviors as they are continually developing the world's perception of you.

Organization

The term <u>multi-tasking</u> has been used to depict a person's ability to do multiple things at the same time. This concept has been challenged as being an impossibility in that the brain can only process one thought at a time. Anyone who examines their own behavior realizes the ineffectiveness of a split focus of attention. With this revelation, it becomes clear that prioritization is a better approach.

Humans are barraged with information. So much so that the consumption of information can paralyze. In business, the expression analysis paralysis is often used as a caution to individuals who may fail to take timely action. As a sales professional you realize you must achieve your objectives and to do so you must take action. Deciding the appropriate action is a function of organizing the deluge of information you acquire.

Individuals have uniqueness when it comes to processing information and interpreting reality. To suggest how another person should organize would be frustrating and ineffective. This is in direct opposition to the purpose of organization which is to achieve greater efficiency and effectiveness through clarity and focus.

There are several observations and best practices that are widely accepted:

- **Planning systems work**: Time is your most important commodity. Proactive planning on how you spend your time should align with your objectives. The habit of planning and organizing at a consistent time during the week reinforces your focus to key objectives.
- **An organized outer appearance conveys power and control:** Think of the office and desk of a CEO and you will likely picture a paper free and clutter free space. They have power and control over their actions, the information does not control them.

- **Organization supports efficiency:** The ability to source and utilize tools and information quickly saves time.
- **Organization can provide both tangible and intangible benefits:** Being organized feels good, looks good, reduces stress and increases confidence.
- **Organization practices evolve:** Best practices get replaced by better practices over time. It is productive to challenge the way you organize time, information and space with the objective to increase your effectiveness.

Better organization leads to greater efficiency. Greater efficiency leads to greater effectiveness. There is no downside to organization.

Time Management

Every one of us is given the same portion of time to use each day. 24 hours to be used however you chose. Your level of success will be determined by how you chose to use your time.

<u>Time management</u> implies that time is something that can be managed. In fact, time moves forward regardless of what we do so there is no management of time but rather the decision process of the activities and durations we chose. Your decisions will determine your destiny.

The application of time management follows the transformation model; that our thoughts lead to choices which then require us to make decisions. Decisions will lead to the development of habits. Our habits are central to our character development. Our character in large part will determine our destiny.

As you consider your choices, you will make decisions on your activities. These decisions should be guided by your vision, mission and goals. But even with this guidance the logic of prioritization can be debated between yourself and others. Discussing your views with peers and managers can be helpful.

Consider a few principles and practical recommendations:

- **Big Rocks:** The concept of Big Rocks is based in the 80/20 principle. It is widely held that 80% of benefits come from 20% of efforts. All efforts take time. It stands to reason that one should always begin planning of time schedules starting with high leverage activities also known as Big Rocks. Time management requires the determination of what you do over what you don't do. You need to determine the Big Rocks, those actions that will reap the greatest rewards.

- **Quadrant 2**: Refers to the principle of proactivity. In his book *7 Habits* of Highly Effective People, Steven Covey refers to the model where he determines the importance and urgency of tasks.

Quadrant 2 is the greatest leverage in personal effectiveness and should be the cornerstone of your time allocation.

	Urgent	Not Urgent
Important	**Quadrant 1** • Crisis • Deadline drive projects • Fire-fighting	**Quadrant 2** • Building capabilities • Maximizing opportunities • Risk management
Not Important	**Quadrant 3** • Interruptions • Most meetings and email	**Quadrant 4** • Trivia • Busy work • Time wasters

- **Eat the Frog:** some activities are distasteful but must be completed. Some of these activities may be pushed to you from supervisors, clients or other positions of power. These items may not be one of your Big Rocks but are important and urgent. Attack procrastination head on and prioritize these actions. The frog is the most difficult thing on your to-do list, the one you are most likely to procrastinate on. Avoiding the frog can drain your energy in the anticipation of the effort. If you must eat two frogs, eat the ugliest one first.
- **Experiment:** Time management is learned through trial and error. The essential process of determining priorities seems straightforward, but with many sales opportunities you will only discover which are better through trial and error. Others may be able to guide and tell you from their experience, but true learning will come from direct experience.

33

- **Maximize:** Many sales gurus speak to the value of adding one more call per day. It is hard to dispute the aggregate benefit of this approach. Effective time management can make this ideal a reality.

Sales professionals realize that time is the most valuable commodity. Your effective use of your time will support you on your quest to achieve personal greatness.

Safety

As organizations mature and grow, they inevitably become aware of the importance of safety. Initially most organizations do not recognize safety as a problem, until they have one or more incidents, which may have dramatic effect on colleagues, clients and the organization.

Organizations are required by law to record their safety statistics and to post those results in a public area within the building. One of the key metrics are the Total Recordable Incident Rate (referred to as TRIR). This metric is profoundly important to many clients and contractors. A high TRIR will prevent participation in certain projects.

Building a culture of safety is the overarching objective. It stands to reason that a culture of safety will unify and guide behaviors. Building a culture of safety is not an easy proposition. The formula starts with awareness education and is then followed by regular reinforcement training.

Knowing that a company has achieved a culture of safety is allusive but one former colleague said it best from my perspective "You know you have a culture of safety when colleagues are wearing their personal protective equipment when cutting their lawn at home."

Sales colleagues are exposed to safety risks in the following areas:

- **Driving:** This is the greatest risk for sales colleagues. The key factor is distracted driving. Other risks include fatique and speeding. Each of these risks are within your control and require self-awareness and focus on your part.
- **Job site visits:** Particular client sites have identified risk due to their business category. Manufacturing, mining, corrections facilities are examples of high-risk sites. Construction sites offer another level of risk. When visiting these facilities, you will be required to obey safety rules and

wear required PPE. Some sites will require orientation training to further mitigate risk.

- **Slips and trips:** in office settings you may be exposed to situations where liquids are spilled on the floor or where trip hazards such as boxes or cords are present. Recognition and action are required on your part.
- **Alcohol:** Sales professionals may be participating in events that include adult beverages. The risk of over-consumption is very real, this can be a career ending risk as DUI offenses will revoke driving privileges.

Beyond the risk that you may encounter in your role, you need to be aware of the risk that exists in the project opportunities you will be selling. Each project, regardless of scope, has some risk. For this reason, you need to conduct a project risk review on every project. Small projects can still have excessive risk to operational colleagues that may determine a no-go bid decision.

When it comes to safety, each colleague plays a critical role in building culture. Do your part to protect yourself and others.

Sales Expenses

Sales professionals will regularly incur expenses as a part of their assignment. The most common expenses include:

- **Travel and living:** Vehicle costs, parking, hotel fees, airfare and meals while traveling.
- **Meals and entertainment:** Meals for customer meetings. Entertainment expenses would include tickets to sporting events, golf and similar.

When advising a sales colleague on sales expense policy I will commonly focus on this question "Would you incur the expense if you were not getting reimbursed?" By this I explain, would the activity lead to greater sales results, thus making the expenditure a wise investment. Making sound decisions on sales expenses is guided by considering the values of integrity and reasonableness. Since not all people have the same interpretations on these values, companies will spell out more specifically the practical guidelines and spending limits.

When you are traveling on business, companies are expected to reimburse you for reasonable cost. <u>Reasonable</u> will generally be viewed as finding competitive prices for lodging, travel and meals. Business travel is not considered a vacation, so you are best served to think like an entrepreneur and realize every expense is a reduction of your company's profit. Managing expenses is everyone's responsibility.

When discussing sales expenses for customer business meetings, most sales colleagues understand the benefit that comes from spending time out of the office with clients. Being allotted time by your customer to meet over breakfast, lunch or dinner usually signals an openness to build a relationship. Building trust with your clients strengthens the bond. It is during these meetings that you shape positive perceptions, resolve issues, build goodwill and move toward agreements.

Most clients are not impressed by how expensive the venue is but rather the value of your contributions that help them achieve their company goals. There are exceptions, but when customers are suggesting extravagant expenses this may signal ingenuous motives. I have more often seen that clients appreciate reasonableness in our behaviors as they see this signaling smart business.

From observing the behaviors of many sales colleagues, I have noted that the majority do not actively utilize sales expenses to leverage relationship development. This is not to suggest that success cannot be achieved through the in-office sales process, rather it is more of an observation that as the sales colleague is received favorably by the client and their organization, trust is growing and with high trust we can more speedily arrive at Win/Win agreements. When customers agree to meet socially, you further build and strengthen relationships of trust.

There are many tools that a sales professional has at their disposal to achieve their objectives. Sales expenses for meals and entertainment with clients is one of those tools. Analogous to many aspects of life, if you use the right tool correctly it will get the job done effectively and efficiently.

Behavior at Events

Sales professionals will attend and participate in many business and social events such as:

- Industry trade shows
- Business conventions
- Training programs
- Team building meetings
- Holiday parties
- Client outings
- Fund raising and charitable events

Every one of these events have a specific mission and the attendees should have an objective with their participation. It is important that you recognize the value to you and your organization for each event. Focus on the purpose of the event and remain fully engaged. Your actions will be observed by many, so be aware that perception is reality.

Some basic tips that should be considered:

- **Be early to events:** This is a sign of respect to the host and presenters. Additionally, it is an opportunity for you to meet with others and build relationships.
- **Be positive**: Be aware of your attitude and recognize the energy you are bringing to the event is influencing others. Negative energy can suck the joy out of events so be mindful of your presence.
- **Be appropriate:** When in doubt, be more professional than less in dress attire. Have a voice, be considerate of others, and stimulate thoughtful conversations. Be serious with your use of time within events.

- **Be careful:** Events have risks, when alcohol is present be mindful of moderation. Celebrations may also lead to embarrassing behaviors that may seem fun and harmless but left unchecked may lead to negative consequences.

Each event allows participants to choose their level of engagement. Some folks may act as hostage while others may be active participants. Some will be followers while some will be leaders. It is in your best interest to be an actively involved leader. By leader, I mean that you are an independent thinker who is aware of your objective. You are appropriately intense and alert. You are aware of the needs of others and you support the mission of the event.

Working at Home/Remote

Sales professionals understand they must deliver results. Whether working in the office, working remote or working from home you are accountable for results. The bottom line is that you determine the best environment to maximize your productivity.

Technology continues to change the way we produce results. With Wi-Fi connectivity virtually everywhere, you have access to company and client information necessary to accomplish tasks.

The challenge of any environment are the distractions. Sales professionals must remain disciplined and focused to the task at hand in order to overcome distractions.

Every working environment has its pros and cons:

- **Working from the Office:** Has the benefit of team collaboration, accessibility of team members, conference rooms, technology, and an environment supportive to organizational culture. The detriment is time spent in commuting and the potential interruptions from colleagues.
- **Working from Home:** Has the benefit of quiet isolation that can support concentration, gaining additional productivity from the elimination of drive time and a potential increase of work/life balance. The downside is the absence of energy derived from the culture of colleagues working in proximity.

In an age when more people are working from home there are practical solutions that support effectiveness:

- Behave like you are at the office. Integrity is best revealed by what you do when no one is watching.
- Be aware of your environment and eliminate distractions.
- Ensure video conferencing represents professionalism. Pay attention to details of background and lighting.

- Be the example which makes others want to be like you. Be on time for calls and complete calls as scheduled.

Regardless of where you perform your work, sales results are derived from interactions with customers. Superior sales professionals develop communication skills and habits that lead to customer confidence. They ultimately increase the <u>quantity</u> of communications, the <u>quality</u> of communications or both.

Face time with customers is essential. Maximizing your time with customers should remain your focus. In person meetings should remain your objective but when you can't get facetime get video conferencing time. In changing times, the objective of human facetime may be replaced with virtual facetime. Accepting this reality, your preference may be impeded but the underlying principles remain that you must:

- Add value to your customers.
- Understand of your customer's goals, problems, needs.
- Think about what you want your customer to think, do or say at the end of the call.
- Have a call plan with an agenda and clear objectives.
- Confirm the time allocated by the customer at the start of the call and complete the call by the designated time.
- Confirm next steps at the completion of the video meeting,

The bottom line is about producing results. Whether working in office or remote, selling face to face or through technology you are accountable for your success.

Section 3 - The Fundamentals

On-Boarding

Companies have recognized the need and benefit of having formal on-boarding programs for new colleagues. It is intuitive that business models become increasingly complex as the business matures and grows. Consequently, it is in the best interest of the colleague and the company to monitor and control the dissemination of knowledge to simplify the complexity.

The on-boarding program for sales colleagues is customized. It is designed to increase your knowledge of organizational processes, tools and resources to aid you in becoming effective and efficient in your assignment. The program provides a guide for the activities that are to be completed within the first 30, 60 and 90 days respectively. The intention of the on-boarding program is to guide and support the training process to its completion and in alignment with the 90-day review and subsequent goal setting.

Successful on-boarding is dependent upon you. The personal leadership mantra "If it is to be, it is up to me" applies to your realization of on-boarding program benefits. History shows that new colleagues want to begin contributing quickly and prove they are adding value. This is natural and welcome. Additionally, it is understood that new colleagues can quickly become overwhelmed with work assignments that will appear to take priority over their on-boarding responsibilities. You are accountable to stay the course and achieve milestones as set forth.

Understanding that you will realize meaningful benefit from the on-boarding program in direct proportion to your personal investment, I encourage that you bring genuine enthusiasm, active listening and feedback to this critical process. The content of the on-boarding program is massive and therefore much of the information can be forgotten if not applied soon after learning. To support absorption, you are strongly encouraged to provide a weekly written summary of your progress and lessons learned. Additionally, research has found

44

that learners have demonstrated a 90% retention rate when they teach others their new knowledge within 3 days[4]. I encourage you to apply both strategies with excellence.

Napoleon Hill stated, "A person cannot exceed mediocrity without the help of others." [5] With this on-boarding program you will have the assistance of your manager, peers and several subject matter experts (i.e. functional leaders in human resources, national accounts, operations etc.). These individuals will support you along your journey. While they are committed to facilitating key parts of your on-boarding experience, they are all carrying full workloads. You can honor their efforts by coming prepared and energized to scheduled meetings and calls.

---

[4] National Training Laboratories, Bethel, Maine
[5] Napoleon Hill, *The Law of Success, pp. xxi (The Penguin Group, New York, 1928)*

Selling Value

In the world of systems sales there are numerous types and sizes of fire alarm, security and low voltage businesses. At one extreme there are large international organizations and on the other extreme there are one-man shops that serve a small client base. Between those extremes are thousands of companies that serve a specific niche. To the industry outsider it may appear that these companies do the same thing in that they sell products and provide services that make those products work within their expected marketing guidelines. Additionally, they provide some level of service support.

Clients have many options to choose from, so how do they decide? Think about your personal buying practices, how do you go about selecting a product or service? Does your practice change for higher value purchases? How much does price play into your selection criteria? Now think about your clients that do not understand the low voltage industry, how will they determine their selection criteria? Do they need help defining value?

So, what does it mean to <u>sell value</u>? Think of a world in which all companies sold the same product and service, in this example all participants would look identical to the customer and therefore a customer could simply accept the company who offered the lowest price. Again, this example is very elementary, but it depicts a state of equilibrium where all competitors are identical. Thankfully for sales professionals this is never true. Because companies are different in many ways, the astute sales professional can present the differentiators and define their unique value.

Ultimately, the customer decides what is of value. You may believe your differentiators should be considered valuable to the customer, but it is their perception that rules. For you to connect with your customer you must understand their goals, problems and needs as a starting point. Secondly, you must demonstrate to the customer how your capabilities and solutions align with their goals, problems and needs. Third, you must build positive perception regarding the key differentiators your products and services possess over your likely competitors to the point that your customer understands the value and therefore desires it.

Opportunities for selling value exist in many areas, some examples include:

- Unique product features that save clients time, reduce their risk or improve their efficiency.
- Extensive experience in a marketplace provides credibility and confidence.
- Resumes' of key personnel establish a higher level of excellence.
- Excellent safety stats indicate a culture of process control.
- Financial stability which reflects staying power and the ability to obtain and manage resources.
- Small business enterprise presents opportunity to meet government requirements for participation.

Outside of these examples is the <u>Value of You!</u> You can be creative and innovative to guide the criteria creation. You can build trust. You can demonstrate confidence and professionalism. If you do these well then price should become a secondary consideration by the customer.

Planning

In your quest to achieve greatness as a sales professional it is imperative that you master the practice of planning. Think for a moment of all the aspects of your sales life that require some form of planning.

- Daily activity planning including a to-do checklist
- Weekly planning and monthly planning
- Annual business planning
- Sales call planning
- Major project strategy planning

As you can see from this list, you need to do quite a bit of planning.

Planning requires an investment in time. All the planning activities listed above require dedicated time and discernment to ensure you are using your most valuable resource (time) effectively. In Steven Covey's book *7 Habits of Highly Effective People* he addresses Habit 3 as <u>Putting First Things First</u> [6]. The lesson speaks to the issue of prioritization and is depicted with the example of 2 empty vases and containers of rocks, gravel, sand and water. In example 1, the person fills the vase with water first then adds sand, gravel and then finds there is no room for the big rocks. When he tries to add the rocks, the water overflows from the vase.

In the second sample the person places the big rocks in first, then adds gravel, then sand and finally, water. All the contents fit! Surprisingly, the second example proved much more efficient and effective.

I refer to this lesson as <u>Big Rocks</u> and it is a well-studied principle. It is also referred to as the Paretto Principle or the 80/20 rule. The key

---

[6] Steven R. Covey, *The 7 Habits of Highly Effective People, pp.154-193 (Simon & Schuster, New York, 2004)*

take-away is that time is your most precious resource, and you are encouraged to prioritize those activities which will provide the greatest benefit.

Planning is a <u>Big Rock</u>. It is a proactive activity which is an activity that is important but not yet urgent (See Habit 1, in *7 Habits of Highly Effective People*). I can assure you with confidence that successful sales colleagues have mastered planning and shift more of their time to working on proactive sales activities (Big Rocks).

These are some of the common planning tools that you will utilize:

- Microsoft Outlook calendar
- Sales call planning worksheet
- Large Account Management Planning (LAMP)
- Major Project Planning worksheet
- Annual Business Plan

Annual Business Plan

As organizations mature, they realize the necessity of implementing planning tools for all aspects of the business. Sales planning is an essential starting point for the overall business plan. It is common for new sales colleagues to struggle in developing their plan so it useful to breakdown both the knowns and unknowns.

One planning tool that I favored was humorously referred to as the <u>Donut Chart</u>. The benefit of this graphic depiction is that it simplifies to one page where your success will be realized. This planning tool takes a wholistic look at three aspects of your market; your existing end-user accounts, targeted end-user accounts and construction accounts which include potential buyers (electrical contractors and general contractors) and potential influencers (architects, engineers and consultants). This tool clearly identifies your Big Rocks and should stimulate your thinking for your weekly activity planning.

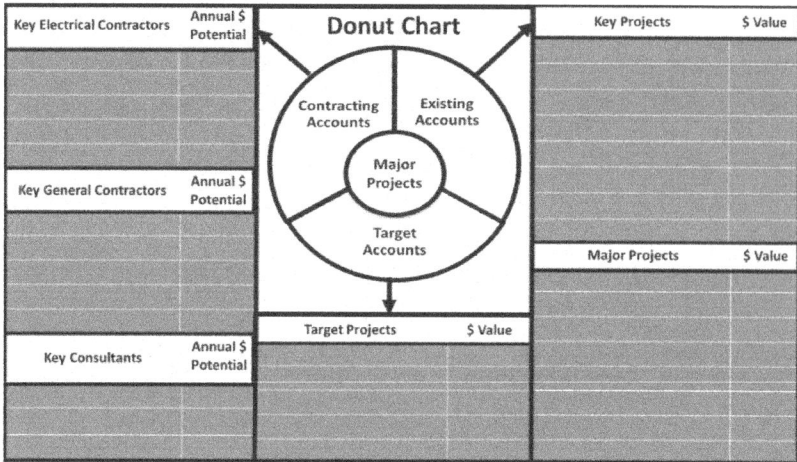

Key Electrical Contractors	Annual $ Potential		Key Projects	$ Value
Key General Contractors	Annual $ Potential			
			Major Projects	$ Value
Key Consultants	Annual $ Potential			

Donut Chart

Contracting Accounts | Existing Accounts

Major Projects

Target Accounts

Target Projects | $ Value

It is beneficial to develop consistent planning routines that form into habit. The habit of planning early in the day, week, and month have great merit. From my personal experience I found the habit of daily planning to be the catalyst for success. For many years I followed a routine of leaving home early and finding a coffee shop near my first appointment where I would review my daily objectives, review to-do lists and consider priorities. This practice of reviewing short-term urgencies and long-term opportunities developed my tactical and strategic thinking. By considering the question of "What orders can I close today?" I was focusing on the short-term actions that would lead to achieving monthly goals. While reviewing project opportunities that were in early stages of the sales cycle, I could proactively plan meetings and presentations that were important but not yet urgent.

As I continued this daily practice and realized the many benefits it was providing, I continued to expand my strategic planning. This resulted in thinking more comprehensively about winning major projects. Formal planning resulted in greater clarity of the opportunity and the sales effort required to develop positive perception with project stakeholders.

As a final caution, do not fall prey to analysis paralysis. Planning is critical but so is the execution of your plan. A good plan without execution equals nothing!

Face Time

The term <u>face time</u> refers to the amount of time you spend face to face with clients. I have found this metric to be useful in determining the probability of long-term success of sales colleagues.

The premise behind face time as a metric is that driving the <u>quantity</u> of sales call activity will naturally result in more closed sales. It should be clear that the <u>quality</u> of the sales call is critically important as well. The quality aspects of your sales calls are addressed in many of the chapters in this book. If you consistently deliver high quality in your sales calls it would stand to reason that increasing your volume would have a positive correlation.

In my first management assignment I became aware of the excessive time my sales team was spending in the office. When exploring why the sales colleagues were spending most of the time in the office it was explained that estimating activities, internal meetings, and follow-up calls were the crux. This became the Genesis for challenging each sales colleague to understand the relation between customer facing activities and sales results.

The predicament that the sales colleagues faced was how they chose to use their time. A wise manager of mine referred to his observation of time management as the <u>Law of Infinite Volume</u>. His explanation of this law was that people will complete tasks within the allotted time. In example, if a person has 8 hours to complete a 4-hour task, they will use 8 hours. On the other hand, if given a 12-hour task that must be done in 8 hours they will accomplish it in the given time. This logic can certainly be argued as naïve, but the high-level interpretation is that with good planning and a sense of urgency an individual can accomplish far more than imaginable.

What is a reasonable face-time goal? Start with the number of hours your customers are available within the week. Do they work 8 to 5? Are they willing to meet for breakfast or dinner? Are they available to meet for relationship building events like golf or sporting events?

The message is that the more hours you have with clients to shape positive perception, to diagnose their problems, to present your solutions and add value to their customers the greater your sales results will be.

Many sales colleagues miss key opportunities to build positive perception and expand relationships. They do not realize the power of face to face human contact in a transaction. They sacrifice the possibility of the magic of human contact for the expediency of a phone call or email. Sales colleagues will be best served if they endeavor to have face to face meetings in the following circumstances:

- **Proposal delivery:** Carefully explain the scope of work, clarifications and the means and methods of the project. Read the customer's body language and ask for feedback. You can expect better dialogue in person than by phone conversation. Many clients prefer to have an email proposal to review prior to discussion, although this is understandable, you should always request to walk them through the details in person.
- **Purchase order award:** Do not miss the opportunity to say, "thank you" and demonstrate appreciation and enthusiasm to begin the project.

Understandably your face time with customers will fluctuate from week to week. When a large project arises, the time spent reviewing project documents, developing cost estimates and proposals can be extremely time consuming. The key take-away is that you must be aware that results logically follow your quality sales efforts.

Start tracking your face time and measure your weekly results. During your weekly planning make every attempt to maximize in-person client meetings. Time and territory management are essential for your success. Plan your days to optimize your sales calls with minimum drive time between calls when possible.

Going to the office does not support your face-time goals. It is a potential landmine for time wasters. Always try for client meetings first thing in the morning.

Another recommendation is to set up shop in the conference room of your large accounts or contractor customers. This has provided great results for sales colleagues. They find that being accessible and visible in their customer's office stimulates awareness of additional opportunities.

Remember that you are the secret weapon for the organization. The energy you create with your clients is the differentiator. Face to face contact should always be the preferred form of customer contact. Additionally, in an age when technology allows for the equivalent of face to face meetings with applications like Skype, Zoom and Teams the temptation to gain efficiencies is prevalent and possibly preferred by some clients. It is in your best interest to push for in person meetings.

Proposal Quality

As a sales professional you are responsible for preparing proposals to solicit business from your clients. Mature organizations have systems that support sales colleagues in the preparation of proposals. The systems provide several benefits:

- They integrate into estimating tools and data bases that ensure proposal pricing is current and accurate.
- They provide for standard formatting to support the organizations branding.
- They include legal terms and conditions that reduce contractual risks.
- They have automated approval ques to ensure large proposals are approved by management prior to tender of offer.

Automated proposal systems provide a significant benefit and helps the sales colleague to stay in their lane by providing proposal guardrails. But for all the automation benefits it is still possible to have a substandard proposal in the view of the client. Some of the areas to be aware of and to avoid include:

- When boilerplate narrative is sent to repeat customers, they will soon recognize that what was once interesting and impressive will become boring and a time waster.
- Proposals that are presented as a bill of material lack clarity of the installation and support services that may be included.
- When the list of exclusions dwarfs the list of inclusions a negative perception may develop by the client. It is not uncommon for the sales colleague to cut and paste a generic exclusion list that has grown to cover every possible problem even those that don't relate to the proposed project.
- No scope of work, or an incomplete scope of work.

You need to maintain awareness that your client will be receiving this document from you and it will represent your professionalism and your attention to detail. You want to be proud of your work and your offer. Ideally, you want to deliver a proposal in person, this is not always possible or practical, but on large and strategic opportunities it is a must.

Some opportunities require a more extensive proposal response in the form of supporting documents. This is common on a Request for Proposal (RFP) solicitation. These responses may require company organization charts, resumes' of key project participants, product information sheets, pricing worksheets, disclosure sheets, etc. To support you on these types of requests, the marketing department has libraries of supporting documents. In some organizations, a proposal group exists to build the tailored proposal for the project requirements.

Ultimately, proposal quality is determined by your customer. Bigger and more is not always better. for example, some contractors require the proposal to only include the wording; "per plans and specifications". In situations like these you will need to use your intuition and reasoning skills to provide a proposal document that is fit for the situation. From another perspective, many clients will equate the massiveness of a proposal binder to commitment and desire. You need to strike the right balance for the situation.

The key take-away is that the quality of the proposal matters! Tools exist to facilitate your efforts, but you are accountable for delivering the appropriate level of quality. If you are to achieve personal greatness you need to be disciplined with every aspect of your position. Take pride in creating high quality proposals. And remember you seldom get a second chance to make a good first impression.

Proposal Follow-up

In your weekly routine you will be estimating work and developing proposals. During the delivery of your proposal it is natural to ask some closing questions like "When do you expect to proceed with this project?" or "Does my proposal meet to your satisfaction?". It is also common that the client will not have firm answers to your closing questions simply because they may not know. Here are a few scenarios to explain why:

- In the <u>private construction bid process</u> you may be offering your proposal to several contractors. They do not control the timing of the decision so the determination of the award date may be affected by whether bids come in within the planned budget. It is further impacted by scope review meetings with contractors to verify completeness of bids.
- In the <u>public bid process</u> several scenarios can exist; bids may be submitted as either private bid openings or public bid openings. At public bid openings the bidders will know immediately how their price compares to all others. In all cases the award will go to the most responsible and responsive bidder who complies with all requirements. Private bid openings may have other criteria which may include "Best Value" consideration that will evaluate each bidder's competencies in key areas rather than lowest bid price.
- In the <u>end-user sales process</u>, the client you are communicating with may not have signing authority and will need to gain approval. Some end user projects require committee approval which prevents firm answers.

In the three scenarios listed, there are numerous variations and factors that impact the decision process. Ultimately, you must learn to ask practical questions under each of these scenarios to obtain information that will lead you to successfully closing the order.

Key information that you need includes:

- Does our proposal fulfill all requirements?
- Do you have any concerns?
- Can we do business together on this project?

With these questions we are attempting to gain confirmation that we are the partner of choice once the project proceeds.

The secondary concern is timing and can be addressed with the following questions:

- When do you expect a decision to be made?
- What is the completion date of the project?
- What is the project schedule?

These questions will serve you well to plan your next steps in securing the order, but many sales professionals have gotten to this point and then blinked. This means they did not follow-up at a key point in time only to find that the project was awarded to a competitor. The message here is that you must be organized, diligent and thoughtful on your follow-up technique. Your client understands that you are in sales and your job assignment is to bring in orders. It is reasonable to ask for orders and ask if there are any objections by the client. It is reasonable to ask if you can follow-up within the next day or week or specific date. It is always good to confirm understanding of timing and next steps.

Here are a few words of caution. It is possible to follow-up too much. You need to have good sense of your client's perception and gain a meeting of minds on follow-up timing. It also helps to have face to face meetings with the purpose of adding value to benefit the client and the project.

In contrast, many sales colleague do not follow-up enough, which is more common. It is critical to understand that your competition is desiring the same thing you are, the thrill of winning the order. In your quest to achieve personal greatness be persistent and smart in follow-up.

Sales Activity Tracking and Management

From my vantage point, sales activity tracking is a weakness in our industry. The possible reasons behind this are:

- Sales professionals may not feel it is important, they may not see how it benefits them in closing more work.
- The input data is often emotional or based on incomplete reasoning.
- Sales colleagues often feel that by reporting certain activity upper management may become curious and therefore more invasive.

Let's cover these items and build a case around why you should persist and track your activity.

Our lives are complicated. By extension, the life of a driven sales colleague is more so. The amount of sales activities that occur each day, week, month and year are staggering. One cannot rely on memory to organize and prioritize critical activities. That was one of the driving forces behind day planners and sales management tools. Sales management tools have evolved significantly to offer an incredible amount of information that can be used to assess the health of the sales colleagues' pipeline. Having accurate and complete information allows for an objective assessment by both the sales colleague and their manager. The objective assessment allows for constructive discussion on activities and behaviors that will lead to greater productivity.

Regardless of whether a manager is evaluating your pipeline, you need to have a disciplined approach to recording your activities and regularly assessing your progress. It is common for a sales professional to go through peak periods where they are swimming hard to keep pace with customer requests. It is very common to become lax in recording during these periods as it is often viewed as lower priority. This is a problem, because inevitably the colleague will lose track of activity for a period and regardless of duration some opportunities may be forgotten and not acted upon. It is essential to have a consistent, disciplined process for both recording and assessing your activity.

Having a sales activity tracker that is accurate and complete provides a tool that can be used to think and plan proactively.

Let's look at some of the proactive uses of an activity tracking tool:

- **Brainstorming:** Identify and qualify opportunities that fit well into your market approach and the organizations competencies. The key here is to be reasonable in the selection process and to follow through with customer contact immediately. A recurring piece of advice is to eliminate the deadwood so as not to have a bloated, unrealistic tool.
- **Scheduling:** When your activity tracking is complete and accurate you can project the timing of sales activities in the future. This includes the time needed to conduct presentations, develop proposals, schedule follow-up calls and close meetings.
- **Forecasting:** An accurate activity tracker facilitates the development of monthly and quarterly forecasts.
- **Metrics Management:** For confirming that your monthly proposal volume is in line with requirements to achieve monthly bookings goal.

Activity tracking and management is an essential function in achieving personal greatness. A best practice for a sales colleague is to review your pipeline report daily and to use it as a prioritization tool. The one most important question to ask is "What can I close today?" Take action to make it happen.

Sales Closure Rate

Closing orders is one of the most exciting and rewarding aspects of sales. It is often a struggle to win an order because of external forces. External forces include customer issues of funding, scope of work and trust. They also include your competition.

Understanding these variables is important to you as you assess your probability of winning any order.

The closure rate in the low voltage industry is approximately 30%. It is expected that new sales colleagues will have a lower closure rate as they develop competencies. Senior colleagues tend to have a higher closure rate because of greater market understanding, repeat business, stronger customer relations and highly developed selling skills.

The importance of understanding your closure rate is a lesson in sales mathematics. As you collect your win/loss data you will begin to understand your business dynamics. This data will help you understand how much input (proposal activity) is required to produce an output (closed orders). Simply stated, if you have a closure rate of 33% you will need to propose 3 times your sales bookings goal. If you have a 20% closure rate you will need to propose 5 times your sales bookings goal.

Sales professionals need to be objective when evaluating metrics because data can be manipulated, it should not be your intent to set a high closure rate as your end goal, but rather to use it as a guide to understand the activity level required to achieve an output goal.

The expression "First be effective then be efficient" is advice that permeates all aspects of business and it is certainly true in sales. Regardless of your tenure in sales, you can be effective with the requisite effort, positive attitude and habits.

One mental model that can be used to demonstrate the achievement of superior sales performance is through the evaluation of a sales colleague's <u>activity level</u> and <u>insight level</u> in this 4-quadrant graphic.

Activity vs. Insight

Low Activity – High Insight	High Activity – High Insight
Low Activity – Low Insight	High Activity – Low Insight

High ← Insight Level

Low — Activity Level — High

The rational assumptions from this model are:

- A sales colleague that has low activity and low insight will struggle and likely fail.
- A sales colleague with high activity but low insight can succeed but will likely have a low closure rate. Akin to <u>spaghetti theory</u>, throw enough against the wall and some will stick.
- A sales colleague with low activity but high insight can succeed if they have a high closure rate. This resembles <u>putting all your eggs in one basket</u>.
- A sales colleague with high activity and high insight will succeed in all cases.

There are multiple paths you may take to achieve your sales goals. Understand your current competencies and build your strategy around your strengths. Remember first be effective then be efficient.

Productivity and Efficiency

Productivity is a measure of output in relation to input. In the world of sales, one of the most common measures is sales bookings (purchase orders received from clients). For example, a sales colleague that produces $10M of sales in a year is viewed as more productive than a sales colleague that produces $1M in a year.

Let's challenge the thinking of productivity by means of an extreme example. If one sales rep acts upon an opportunity for $10M and closed this singular order and another sales representative closed $10M through 200 orders are they equally productive? While the first person was certainly more efficient, they were equally productive.

Most sales professionals and managers see the benefit of efficiency, but they also realize that they first must be productive. The expression first be effective then be efficient rings true as a practical mantra. Sales colleagues entering a new organization must go through the process of building a backlog of proposals. They can only build backlog through identifying opportunities, qualifying opportunities, conducting sales presentations and tendering proposals.

The average closure rate in the low voltage systems industry is approximately 30%. Very successful sales colleagues that have deep client relationships, highly developed markets and strong strategic planning will have much higher closure rates. Developing sales colleagues will naturally have lower closure rates as they ramp up in their development of client relationships and territory.

Once you know your closure rate you can determine what your monthly proposal volume needs to be. By the previous example, the established sales colleague with a closure rate of 50% may be more efficient than a developing sales colleague with a 20% closure rate, but they could have the same productivity. The developing colleague will need to have significantly more sales proposal activity to deliver the same output.

For a developing sales colleague, <u>sales call activity is a key productivity metric</u>. Time and territory management is critical for all sales colleagues who aspire to achieve greatness. Additionally, you must bring an unstoppable energy to maximize your call per day productivity. Some of the best advice I can give is to eliminate time wasters, stay out of the office, increase face time with clients and work long hours.

Proposal Activity

Annual Quota	Monthly Quota	Monthly Proposal volume @ 33% close rate	Monthly Proposal volume @ 20% close rate	Monthly Proposal volume @ 10 % close rate
$1,200,000	$100,000	$300,000	$500,000	$1,000,000
$2,400,000	$200,000	$600,000	$1,000,000	$2,000,000
$3,600,000	$300,000	$900,000	$1,500,000	$3,000,000
$4,800,000	$400,000	$1,200,000	$2,000,000	$4,000,000

Higher Efficiency   Same Effectiveness to Achieve Goal

Section 4 - Strategies and Tactics

Go-to-Market Approach

As a sales professional you assume the responsibility to develop your personal business plan which will detail how you intend to accomplish your objectives., you define your Go-To-Market approach. The low voltage systems market is enormous, virtually every commercial building uses products or services that you can provide. Many considerations go into deciding which markets are best for you, and where you add the greatest value for your customers. Ask yourself the following questions:

- Which vertical markets do you know best?
- Which vertical markets does your organization have the best operational competency?
- Which product lines does your organization excel in?
- In which markets do you face strongest/weakest competition?
- Are their opportunistic markets as a result of political, social or environmental changes?
- Which markets offer recurring service business?
- Which markets offer greater profitability?

There are countless strategies and approaches that can be successful. Your success depends heavily on your ability to determine your Go-To-Market approach.

Most industry participants prefer to sell directly to the end-user of the products and services. The benefit of this approach is that you can emphasize your unique value. It is generally believed that price becomes a secondary consideration in many deals and that end-users (owners) will often pay a premium for perceived quality.

End-user selling will require you to invest a significant effort in identifying and qualifying opportunities. Finding new customers is a key part of your assignment and requires dedicated blocks of time planned into your week. At the same time there will be some opportunities that will come your way that will require reactive response. These are welcome and can aid in your success. You are best served when we have a receptive end-user that cares about quality and values working with world class organizations.

The other common market approach is selling through contractors as part of a construction project. This approach can produce equally successful outcomes. Contractor selling is significantly more complicated and requires strong relationships of trust with the industry participants. It is very rewarding when you have relationships, and your competition does not. Most sales colleagues in our industry transact in the bidding process. They do not have established relationships with the contractors which hampers their ability to sell value. Your high trust relationships with contractors allows you to no longer rely on winning projects based on low price strategies.

Why would a sales colleague consider a focus on the construction bid market? For one reason, there is low marketing cost. You don't have to search for customers as the contractors have already identified an on-going stream of opportunities. Now you only need to outperform your competition with superior responsiveness, quality, professionalism and integrity. The sweet spot of selling in the construction market is Strategic Project Selling. Not all projects are strategic. A strategic project is one that is identified to possess the ideal fit of project requirements. It aligns with your key competencies and the strategic players with which you have strong relationships. Strategic players include:

- The owner/ end-user
- Construction Manager
- Electrical Contractor
- Architect
- Consultants
- Other influencers (fire inspectors, specialty contractors)

The premise of Strategic Project Selling is that you must gain positive affirmation from each participant that you are the optimal choice. This is a challenging task. You can still win without unanimous support, but your odds of doing so will be reduced. There are many sub-strategies, but all include making sales calls, doing capability presentations and building trust. These all take time, and they are best accomplished when they are done proactively and long before bid day. Most Strategic Projects are very large in scope, highly complex and high in dollar value. Your selling efforts need to begin very early in the process to unify and align the participants to your value proposition.

Regardless of which market approach you take, you will be served well by being proactive. Steven Covey's *7 Habits of Highly Effective People* describes Habit 1 as <u>Be Proactive</u> [7], to work on things that are important but not yet urgent. Through effective long range planning you will be able to shape perception through a series of sales calls that will lead you to a successful project win.

[7] Steven R. Covey, *The 7 Habits of Highly Effective People*, pp. 73-101 *(Simon & Schuster, New York, 2004)*

Prospecting

Once you have determined your Go-To-Market approach you can build out your prospecting plan. The prospecting plan is analogous to prospecting for gold, as it sets out to find prospective clients. When discussing prospecting, we will refer to the identifying and qualifying stages of the sales cycle.

The first stage of prospecting is identifying potential clients who will benefit from your products and services. How do you determine who those clients might be? Think back on your Go-To-Market questions:

- Which vertical markets do you have experience and success in? Identify similar businesses.
- Which businesses are growing or expanding in your market? Check business journals.
- What current trends are occurring politically, socially, environmentally that will affect business needs?
- Where are the aging systems in your market? General observation and networking can provide insight.

This brainstorming exercise will produce a lengthy list of potential clients. Next you will need to contact the key individuals within those organizations.

Contacting the prospective client can be achieved through a phone call, social media, email, or face to face contact. All methods can work but reality depicts that the hit rate with this approach is low. This is not intended to be a negative but rather the observation that you must be prepared for a marathon of effort. As you might imagine, the likelihood that your potential client's needs and timing will match with your desire for a more immediate sales opportunity is expectedly low. The good news is that you are planting seeds today that you will harvest over many years. Prospecting is a numbers game.

Determining the point of contact within an organization will be predicated on your objective and assignment. As a systems integrator, you have so many offerings and therefore it is critical to narrow your focus and select your appropriate entry point to the organization. Failure to do so can lead to overly complex messaging that will likely prevent individuals from assimilating how you can assist them with their business needs. Large organizations have multiple decision makers and influencers which include:

- President
- Director of Security
- Operations Manager
- Director of Vendor Management
- Purchasing Manager
- Human Resources Manager
- Director of Engineering
- Director of Nursing
- Director of IT
- Chief Information Officer
- Chief Financial Officer

It certainly helps if you can determine some of the pressing needs of the organization in advance. This will allow you to better target the right entry point. You can determine much from annual reports which will often define the organizations strategic objectives for the year. Other publicly available data may provide reasonable intelligence to pique some interest. The key ask is for an introductory meeting to learn about the client's goals, problems and needs. The secondary objective is to present an overview of yourself and the organization. Clients often see the broader scope of how you can help their organization and thus facilitate a meeting with the larger team of stakeholders. Your key objective is to gain an audience. Your next objective is to deliver your capabilities presentation and build positive perception.

As a result of your prospecting efforts you will conclude whether there is an opportunity now, in the future or unlikely. As you qualify the opportunities there is a helpful acronym to reflect upon, it is **WoMAN**:

- **W**illingness: Does the client want to proceed with the project?
- **M**oney: Is there an approved budget?
- **A**uthority: Does the individual you are dealing with have the authority to issue a purchase order?
- **N**eed: Is there a compelling reason why this project needs to happen?

Prospecting is heavy lifting, and it is essential for a sales professional's development of a marketplace. As you progress you will find things will get easier. Sales leads will be provided by your existing clients and industry product partners. Additionally, trade associations provide forums to meet potential customers with established needs.

Contractor Selling

To succeed in selling to contractors it is beneficial to walk in their shoes. Think about the business model of a contractor, whether a general contractor, electrical contractor or a specialty contractor. They are participating in a bid environment, where price often trumps value. Since many of the participants are viewed as <u>equal</u> competitors they are often competing on lowest price. The top tier contractors have financial strength, but the risk of one major project problem, mistake or lawsuit looms large to take them out of business. Being a contractor is not for the weak of heart. What are the goals, problems and needs of a contractor?

- **Goals:** To make a profit, to complete projects on time and on budget, to satisfy client expectations and collect their cash including retainage.
- **Problems:** Managing resources, on-time delivery, effective project leadership, cooperation between trades, managing uncertainty and unknowns, managing risk, talent management and scope creep.
- **Needs:** Strong team members with proven capabilities and positive attitudes, cash flow, partnership and trust

When you analyze the goals, problems and needs of a contractor and compare those to an end user you will realize that they are different. Consequently, their decision drivers very different. The long-term benefit of the low voltage system is not a concern of the contractor. They are principally responsible to provide a working system that meets a performance criterion and provides a warranty for a one-year period. Since the contractor will not be the end-user of the product, they do not value product features, functions and their implied benefits.

Contractors care about making a profit. They can achieve this through negotiating the best deal from the system suppliers (you and your company). They can also improve their project profitability through efficiency in field labor. If a supplier has a product that can save the contractor labor units (time), it may benefit the contractor to pay more for that technology. This has been realized with innovative installation methods, smaller conduit requirements, integrated systems, wireless technology and subcontracting various specialty scopes of work.

Contractors meet with countless numbers of suppliers, all of whom are trying to pitch their unique value propositions. How do they decide on who to select? How would you decide? When you have many offers and they all look very similar, lowest price then becomes a key determining factor. What if you are <u>not</u> the low bid, what do you do? Let's discuss some strategies that work:

- **Build long term relationships**: As you might imagine, this does not help you if you are bidding a project with a new contractor, but this is absolutely the best strategy if you intend to sell in the construction market long term. It requires consistency in calling on contractor accounts, timely and excellent follow-up, excellent project performance and friendly cooperation. Do this well and over time you will build trust. Contractors will pay a preference for you and your company once you have established yourself as the premier talent. When they face a situation where they cannot pay a preference, they will give you <u>last look</u> to accept the job at the market price.

- **Get the Owner/ End-user to request you:** Even when the contractor is making the purchasing decision, the owner can require the contractor to provide the product or company they feel is in their best interest. The owner still has ultimate decision power if they choose to use it.

- **Get the Construction Manager to request you:** Like the owner request, the construction manager loses nothing by making the same requirement. So why would they do it? Again, this tactic works if you have built a relationship with the construction manager and they can see the true value of you and your organization over the rest of your competition.

72

High trust relationships are key. When contractors trust both your character and your competence you are positioned to win big and often. During my sales career in the I benefited from great relationships with contractors. This was exemplified in both the simple examples of being treated different and better than my competitors to the extreme examples of closing major sales orders over breakfast.

Like many other aspects of life success comes after paying your dues and in the process demonstrating your value. This lesson applies to contractor sales as well. It is important to understand that if you are committed to achieving greatness in this market you must consistently outperform every one of your competitors. You must outwork them, out-think them and be a business partner that the contractors respect, trust and like. You can sense when you have gained status with contractor accounts because they have become your friends.

End-User Selling

In contrast to contractor selling where the customer (contractor) is much less emotionally attached to the product, end-user selling is heavily slanted in the other direction. For this reason, value will take precedence over price. Your value proposition to an end-user is different than that of a contractor. Let's compare:

Value proposition for contractor	Value proposition for End-user
• Competitive price/low price • Product meets all project requirement • Product offers economies in installation • You possess more and better resources • Proven track record of completing similar projects • Knowledgeable in contracting law • Robust safety program • Engineering department support • Project management excellence	• World leader in low voltage/ integrated systems • Mission of service excellence • Proven track record of performance • Best trained specialists to optimize product performance • Customized service offerings to protect your investment • Future-proof products with migration strategies for expansion • Commitment to partnership and continuous improvement through quarterly business reviews • Technologies that maximize system performance and up-time

The contractor sale is focused on a singular project endeavor. Your performance on each individual project sets the tone for negotiating future work and shapes an overall perception of you and your organization. The end-user sale is founded on the objective that parties are entering into a long-term relationship. Granted, if the project is small in scope and price, the view of a long-term commitment may not carry as much weight. On large opportunities the end-user wants to be sure they are partnering with the right organization because the change out of building systems can become extremely costly and challenging. This is particularly relevant to end-users that have an aggressive growth strategy.

The following are the end-user's goals, problems and needs:

- **Goals:** Protect the people and assets of the business, improve safety and security, upgrade obsolete technology, risk mitigation and improve colleague productivity.
- **Problems:** Systems are inoperable, current service provider is not performing to requirements and operational costs are too high.
- **Needs:** Need a trusted partner with high character that is highly competent, technology that will meet today's requirements and adapt well to future needs, peace of mind and confidence in their decision.

Your challenge is to win the hearts and minds of the end-user. Each end-user client will have their own opinions and beliefs that you must uncover. You will need to build trust and handle objections. It is your communications skills, attitude and professionalism that will be on display and evaluated by the client. Remember that you will likely be competing against rival companies, so you must be astute regarding how you relate and connect with clients. There have been many studies on the psychology of selling. Tony Alessandra wrote the book *Non-Manipulative Selling* [8] where he describes his theory that selling is _not_ aligned with the golden rule which professes "Do unto others as you would have others do unto you." In non-manipulative selling you need to sell to your clients the way they want to be sold to, not

---

[8] Tony Alessandra, Phil Wexler, Rick Barrera, *Non-Manipulative Selling,* *1987*

the way you would want to be sold to. Tony Alessandra describes four personality types: Director, Relater, Socializer and Thinker. These categories are defined by the level of directness of their communication style and their level of openness in sharing their thoughts and feelings. The chart below describes these four personality styles.

Relater	Socializer
• Low directness of communication • Open to sharing thoughts and feelings	• High directness of communication • Open to sharing thoughts and feelings
Thinker	**Director**
• Low directness of communication • Self-contained to sharing thoughts and feelings	• High directness of communication • Self-contained to sharing thoughts and feelings

By better understanding your client's personality style and preference you can better develop comfort and trust with them. Your task is to align your communication style with that of the client. Mastering the ability to diagnose your client's predominant personality style does not guarantee success but it is one more tool in your toolbox. Again, everything counts.

Architects and Engineers

Architects and their team of engineers are essential to the construction process of any new building or renovation project. Architects are selected by the owner to lead the design effort. They provide administrative support functions through key stages of the construction process which include:

- Project Inception
- Design development
- Construction documents
- Project administration
- Project acceptance.

The architect will also hire a team of specialty engineers to design the structural, mechanical and electrical systems. The knowledge required to design a building and to engineer every aspect of its component parts requires the effort and input from many highly competent individuals.

Low voltage systems are required in commercial buildings. Fire alarms are required based on occupancy type. Sound and communications may include telephony, intercom and paging. Security may include intrusion detection, video monitoring and access control. Mass notification systems, shooter detection, clock systems and data cabling systems are all systems that may be required on a project. Clearly, it is difficult for the most talented sales professional to have competency in all the features, functions and benefits of these numerous systems. It is highly unlikely for an architect or engineer to design these systems without assistance.

As buildings and systems become more complex, architects and engineers need support from industry specialist like yourself to educate and guide them on technology solutions that provide the building owner with optimal benefit. The electrical engineer is contracted by the architect to develop a set of drawings to detail the scope of work and device locations of all electrical systems, including low voltage systems. They are also required to develop a specification manual that details acceptable manufacturers materials, installation means and methods and any other information they deem necessary to communicate project requirements.

Electrical engineers are astute businesspeople who understand they need critical input from industry participants to remain current on product trends and installation materials. They welcome such professionals to educate and train their junior engineers and, in some cases, may even accept your offer to design selective systems.

Listed below are some tactics for engaging with electrical engineers:

- Request an introductory meeting with the lead engineer to establish relationship and discuss capabilities.
- Offer to conduct a Lunch & Learn for the electrical engineer's team.
- Offer to write the guide specification for the relevant systems on a project.
- Offer to layout and design the systems on a project.

These tactics are not new, in fact they were common for many product providers. Over the last two decades much momentum has been lost by product manufacturers in building relationships of trust with electrical consultants. The time is always ripe for a motivated sales professional to develop a coverage strategy in this area. If you decide to deploy a Go-To Market strategy in the construction market, you would be wise to include a goal to develop relationships with the top electrical engineers in your marketplace.

Many low voltage product manufacturers have marketing positions that take the lead is educating and supporting the consulting community. This approach has been a response to the void left by the sales professionals. The fact remains that the consulting community has unmet needs, and the astute sales professional can capitalize upon this market segment. To provide an example, while I was developing my understanding of the roles and goals of the consultants, I met with a small architectural firm to discuss a medical office building they were designing. I provided a brief presentation on life safety systems, product features and a guide specification. Several months later I was contacted by electrical contractors who advised me that the project documents issued for bidding had instructed all bidders to contact me for the life safety scope of work as the sole acceptable provider. Although this event is not commonplace it does provide evidence that calling on consultants can have a direct effect in winning orders.

Architects and Engineers perform an essential role in the construction community. It is imperative that they perform their work with accuracy and excellence for the contractors to succeed and for the end-user to benefit. You can provide consultants with vital support that will help them achieve success. By helping architects and engineers succeed you will be rewarded for your service.

Authorities Having Jurisdiction

The term Authorities Having Jurisdiction, commonly referred to as AHJs is an individual or individuals who interpret and enforce codes and standards. If you are selling fire alarm systems and life safety solutions, you will become very familiar with this terminology referenced in the NFPA code books (National Fire Protection Association). Within your marketplace you will discover that the person who has jurisdiction will be defined by the state charter. You will find that there are local fire marshals, county fire marshals and state fire marshals. Additionally, some localities have plan examiners and fire inspectors. All these individuals will be respected as the AHJ when involved.

AHJs do not buy anything from you, yet they are a project participant that wields incredible power. If you are offering to sell a fire alarm system to a client, regardless of whether it is a new construction project or a renovation project, you will need to submit drawings to the AHJ for approval. The AHJ has a set of published standards that they will adhere to in the review process. This typically includes the NFPA code adopted for a particular year. It would stand to reason that the sales professional is equally knowledgeable with the adopted codes so that he is offering the client a system that meets such code and, therefore, is able to be approved.

It is not uncommon that the AHJ may interpret code sections differently than you are therefore it is beneficial to establish a harmonious professional relationship with them. You offer a significant added value to your client if you can dialogue with the AHJ and gain pre-approval prior to submitting your proposal. I can't overstate the value of having a trusting relationship with the various AHJs. It might not help you sell the project to the owner or contractor, but a poor relationship could cost you severely in project cost overruns if the AHJ becomes difficult.

These are examples of how the fire marshal can impact project cost:

- Fire inspector determines the fire alarm device spacing is inadequate and requires additional equipment.
- During acceptance testing the Fire inspector walks off the job if minor issues arise (i.e. product warranty) resulting in the need to reschedule stakeholders and lost time.
- Fire inspector will not accept certified pre-test and insists on full retest of the entire system.
- Fire inspector will not accommodate continuous testing through completion, rather allotting small blocks of testing time.

On the flip side, the sales professional that builds the trusting relationship with the AHJ and creates a partnership with the project stakeholders can avoid most problems and create an excellent experience for all. Building trust with the AHJ takes time and effort, it does not happen with one introductory sales call, but it also does not take years. The following are suggestions to moving up the trust ladder:

- Request an introduction meeting with the AHJ, learn about their process and pain points.
- Find reasons to discuss code interpretation on a project being developed.
- Offer to conduct a product or code training session to AHJ and associates.
- Submit testing reports to validate project has been certified for AHJ acceptance test.
- Conduct planning meeting with AHJ to review requirements and deliverables.

AHJs are public servants, they serve a necessary role in maintaining public safety. We need each other to help achieve the end-user's goal of building occupancy. You play an important role as the face of the organization that establishes a level of professionalism and excellence. In your quest to achieve sales greatness, this is a value-add sales function that will separate you from the pack.

Competitive Assessment

Think about a sales world where a customer asks for your product or service and you have no competition. Imagine what this would do to the way you think about creative solutions, pricing, urgency and stress. Without competition would it be possible to achieve personal greatness? Competition forces us to get better.

Like it or not competition is here to stay. Most businesses have procurement guidelines that require them to solicit multiple bids for major purchases. Most buyers see the benefit of obtaining at least three supplier prices to ensure they are receiving fair and competitive pricing. Because of business norms, we expect to have competition as a regular course of business.

Knowledge of the competitive field is a learned competency. It comes from numerous data points that are obtained from client feedback, anecdotal information, business associations, fellow colleagues and industry publications. Knowing your major competitors is important for you in developing your Go-To Market strategy. Additionally, it is also your keen understanding of the strengths and weaknesses of players within those companies. Once you understand your competition you can effectively develop your sales call action plan.

It is common to conduct a competitive analysis on an annual basis. Most businesses intuitively see the benefit of analyzing their competition to understand their market strategy. One method used to assess the competition is a SWOT analysis. This tool uses a 4-quadrant worksheet that identifies the following organizational assessments:

- Internal strengths
- Internal weaknesses
- External opportunities
- External threats

This exercise helps clarify how and where to compete in the marketplace. It will guide decisions on where to invest and focus resources in order to excel over the competition. It also highlights capabilities that need to be leveraged and accentuated.

Most sales colleagues know intuitively which competitors they match up best against. They know their own competitive advantage and think they know that of their competitor. With this knowledge the insightful sales colleague builds a communication plan to shape positive perception of their value proposition. It is also important to remember that the sales professional can be the force multiplier for any company. A sales professional with great communication skills working for an inferior competitor can outsell a sales professional with average communication skills working for a superior company. Know the people you are competing against, learn what they do well set your bar to surpass them.

	Helpful	Harmful
Internal	Strengths **S**	Weaknesses **W**
External	Opportunities **O**	Threats **T**

Major Projects - Complex Sales

For a project to be considered a <u>Major Project</u> it must carry a significant benefit to the organization's business. That benefit might be a very large revenue opportunity, a strategic client that might provide expansion nationally or globally, or it may be the opportunity to execute a complex technology solution. You and the business are motivated to win these projects as they are game changers. From a sales perspective, working on major projects can be both challenging and exciting. They require expanded strategic thinking because of their complexity.

Every major project is a unique undertaking. Since major projects are large in scope, owners must create a budget for a capital expenditure. These projects may take many years to complete. The design effort is extensive, and the systems design may progress for over a year. Major projects are a lengthy process, but it is this lead time that works in your favor if you use such time wisely.

Major projects require the development of a project sales strategy. Templates exist to guide your analysis and planning of your strategy. The key elements of building your sales strategy include:

- **SWOT analysis:** What are your strengths, weaknesses, opportunities and threats?
- **Project players:** Who are the decision makers and influencers? What is your relationship with each player (positive, neutral, negative)?
- **Competitive analysis:** Who is your competition? What are their strengths and vulnerabilities? How do you outperform them?
- **Internal resources:** Who is on your sales team? What are their responsibilities? Who is the team leader?
- **Key strategies and action plans:** Based on your analysis, what are the key sales activities that will create positive

perception of your ability to satisfy the goals, problems and needs of the key stakeholders?

Creating a project strategy takes a concerted effort by the team, but it starts with the leadership of one sales colleague who accepts ownership as team leader.

The responsibility of the team leader includes:

- Communicating the vision and objectives of the project.
- Facilitating and managing activities with the project team.
- Coordinating engagements and communications with the project players.

The blessing of major projects is that you have plenty of time to influence the outcome through a series of sales activities. Most sales activities in the early stages do not take excessive time. These activities are important but not yet urgent (Habit 1 from *7 Habits of Highly Effective People*). The highly organized sales colleague can effectively plan sales calls over this extended period that are creative, add value and build positive perception. But the flip side is more commonly true, that many sales colleagues do not use the early stages effectively and essentially try to cram sales activities in the late stages. I encourage you to be in the rare minority that has the discipline to build a comprehensive strategy, collaborate with the team and local leadership and execute on the plan. Remember your competitors have the same time available with which to develop and execute their strategy. Make sure you are first out of the gate and get a leg up on the competition!

Section 5 - Skills, Knowledge and Continuous Improvement

Training and Development

To achieve personal greatness you must be prepared for numerous challenges. The expression "What got us here, won't get us there" directly relates to the topic of training and development. To realize your dream you must get better, you must adopt the practice of continuous improvement. The practice of continuous improvement came about in the era of total quality management. It originally focused on the manufacturing sector with an intent to eliminate waste in operational processes. In the context of sales, continuous improvement is about getting better in every possible aspect as a sales agent and as a human being. It is about becoming more effective as a sales professional by being more efficient (eliminating waste) in your selling efforts.

Training and development can be viewed as an input/output relationship. Training is the input activity of <u>instructing</u> colleagues on new knowledge and concepts. This includes the knowledge of products, markets and selling skills. Additionally, training is the practice of <u>applying</u> this new knowledge thereby transforming it into improved competencies.

Your personal development is the output from training. Human resource experts have asserted that there is a formula for colleague development referred to as the 70/20/10 model. 70% of development comes from on the job experience. 20% comes from mentoring and coaching while 10% comes from formal training. The greatest impact in your development happens every day in the trenches. By raising your awareness and intentionality you can show rapid improvement in your competencies.

The second learning dimension comes from mentoring and coaching. This will be provided primarily by your manager. It is in your best interest to seek regular feedback and coaching. Most sales colleagues do not take advantage of this benefit. You are best served to persist and request one-on-one coaching sessions.

The third learning dimension is formal training. This includes reading, research, podcasts and webinars. Many of these training resources can be incorporated into your daily routines.

In his highly acclaimed program called *Lead the Field*, Earl Nightingale develops a concept called the <u>Strangest Secret</u>[9]. The essential message is that we become what we think about. Our minds are like fertile soil ready to facilitate growth once seeds of thought are planted. My recommendation is to think about how you can get better. Develop your growth plan and share it with your manager. Align your plan with your vision and remember that your personal development should be intentional rather than accidental.

Continuous Improvement is a natural process:

- **Diagnose your development needs:** Talk with your manager to determine your competencies that are under-developed.
- **Create your development plan:** Select 2 or 3 focal areas at a time. Do not attempt to boil the ocean!
- **Execute the plan:** Remain disciplined and tenacious.
- **Track progress:** Record the specific areas in which you gained new knowledge or skills.
- **Repeat the process.**

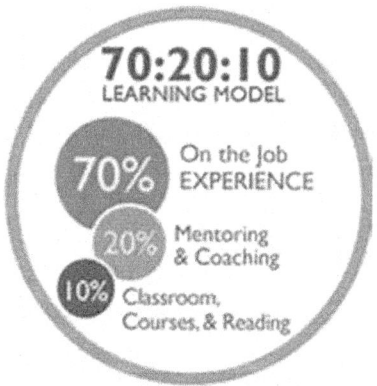

---

[9] Earl Nightingale, *The Strangest Secret, audio cd, 1986 (Nightingale-Conant, Chicago)*

Product Knowledge

The expression "knowledge is power" certainly seems logical. As you observe many aspects of society it does appear that knowledge provides an advantage and strength to the individual who has it. In the low voltage systems industry, the same can be said for the sales colleague who has superior product knowledge. They have an advantage over their competition and the power to offer superior value to customers.

For a sales colleague that is new to the low voltage industry the learning curve is steep. Take comfort in knowing that many have preceded you on this same journey. Or as often quoted "The journey of a thousand miles begins with the first step." An important first step is to understand the basics about the products you will be offering. The following are questions to consider:

- Why are these products needed?
- What needs do these products satisfy?
- How do these products function?
- What benefits do these products provide?

Asking and answering these questions will keep you grounded in customer centric thinking. Remembering that you must always understand and confirm the customer's goals, problems and needs before you can recommend a product and its features, functions and benefits. As a consultant to your customer you must diagnose before you prescribe.

As a developing sales colleague your ability to offer solutions will be affected by your overall knowledge of the products. You can overcome shortcomings by soliciting support from senior sales associates, project engineers or manufacturers' representatives. As you develop product knowledge and gain confidence in presenting features, functions and benefits you become more effective and efficient. You require less assistance. You become more comfortable in handling product application questions and the client's perception will be positively shaped.

All companies have a market niche in which they perform best. Understand what your niche is and learn those products that best fit.

The process of acquiring product knowledge will be the result of the following activities:

- Reading product literature and marketing data.
- Watching training videos and webinars.
- Meeting with product partners and participating in formal training programs.
- Working with your operations teams to see how products perform in actual projects.
- Conversations with customers and colleagues that will test your understanding.

Your learning challenge is simple, but it is not easy. You must be determined to learn and retain knowledge. One of the best ways to facilitate knowledge retention is to teach what you have learned to others within 72 hours. I encourage you to adopt this practice with a fellow colleague, manager, family member or friend.

Estimating

Estimating is an essential function within the building trades industry. Many organizations have full time estimators that develop budgetary prices and firm fixed price bids. In the low voltage industry, the estimating responsibility is handled by the sales colleague or an estimator. The decision as to which direction the business takes is dictated by management philosophy, skill sets of the sales team and the market activity level.

Estimating is a developed competency. It requires the person doing the estimate to have a complete understanding of the customers' requirements, determining a solution and then determining the cost of that solution. This sounds like a straightforward exercise until you realize the variability that can occur within these three steps.

Understanding customer requirements: When you engage with the customer you are collecting information about their goals, problems and needs. This will require you to probe for understanding to achieve a meeting of the minds. It is beneficial to provide tell back of your understanding to the client. Humans have inaccurate memories, so it is essential that the sales professional clarify understanding in writing.

Determining a solution: Solution considerations may be impacted by the following:

- Available technologies
- Physical installation challenges
- Safety and environmental factors
- Labor union requirements
- Work hours
- Product performance limitations

Additionally, the level of quality may be considered where there will be a Good/ Better/ Best offering.

Determining the cost: Cost estimating is a process. Most organizations have a process in place to function as a quality assurance program. Depending on their business practice and model, organizations adopt an estimating methodology of either parametric, cost-up or list price with discounting. As companies mature, they continue to refine their approach to ensure estimates are aligned with historic performance metrics.

Contingency: Variability exists in the three previously noted stages. It is advisable that the estimator include a contingency line in the cost estimates to cover risks that are both foreseen and unforeseen.

Listed below are the pros and cons of a sales colleague versus an estimator performing the estimating function:

Sales Pros	Sales Cons
• Communication directly with the client minimizes misinterpretation of project scope • Motivated to scrutinize cost • Accountability remains with the sales colleague	• Estimating function reduces sales face-time opportunities • Sales colleagues may not be efficient or skilled at estimating

Estimator Pros	Estimator Cons
• A dedicated estimator is more efficient and competent • An estimator can leverage information between the sales team • An estimator improves sales colleague productivity	• Knowledge transfer from sales colleague may lose important information. • Not emotionally vested in winning or losing project • May not be motivated to find innovations for reducing cost

Regardless of who prepares the estimate, the sales colleague must possess a comprehensive understanding of the project scope, project objectives, solution and cost estimate in order to convey confidence to the customer. Both approaches have merit and can work equally well.

Communication Skills

Sales professionals help customers achieve their goals, solve their problems and provide for their needs. To accomplish these objectives, you can:

- Listen, observe and discern what your customer is interpreting.
- Synthesize the information and to retell your understanding.
- Analyze situations.
- Employ creative thinking to develop solutions.
- Document and memorialize conversations.
- Interpret emotions and provide empathic responses.
- Negotiate to Win/Win contracts.

Communication skills are now and will continue in the future to be a critical differentiator in your journey to success. Observe other sales colleagues or business professionals and analyze their performance. Ask yourself these questions, "Would I buy from them?" or "Do I trust them?" Notice other signals including body language, professional appearance, articulation, confidence, energy and organization. This exercise reinforces the expression "First impressions make lasting impressions."

Many people have a negative perception of salespersons. This is a result of bad experiences due to poor communication skills, poor motives or both. Think of your experiences. Do you recall when you felt pressured by the salesperson because they were more concerned about making a sale than truly understanding your goals, problems or needs?

When it comes to communication success you will be best served to check your attitude. The sales training program (Acclivus) refers to the concept of <u>integrity of intent</u>[10], which means to absolutely serve the customer. If your product or service is not the ideal fit, be honest

---

[10] Acclivus Corporation, *R3 Sales Excellence, 2003*

with the customer and provide alternative guidance, which may include using a competitor's service.

Secondly, you can never undervalue professionalism. This includes the first impression stuff plus being prepared and organized. It is essential that you have a written sales call plan that identifies your objective and strategy for the meeting. A common element within many communications is the use of presentation materials. When this is the case, the sales professional must understand the benefit and limitations of information. Be aware or the audience, their attention span, their time conflicts and their interest.

Great communicators achieve superior results when they have the right balance of fact finding, inquiry and diagnosis before prescribing a solution. They do not presume answers before the customer explains their goals, problems or needs. Great communicators focus on building positive customer perceptions through reasonable, timely and high-quality responses.

Regardless of your current skill level, your goal should be to improve as a professional communicator. Ask for feedback from your manager, peers and even your customer. As your communications skills improve, you will find your ability to serve your customers will be enhanced and your effectiveness as a sales professional will improve.

Presentation Skills

I recall attending an American Society for Industrial Security dinner meeting around the year of 1984. After dinner the keynote speaker was introduced and commenced with his presentation. Over 35 years later I cannot recall the name of the speaker nor the topic he spoke of, but what I do remember is the feeling of what presentation excellence looks like. The details I can recall were the poise and confidence the speaker projected. His physical traits of strong body language. His mastery of projecting his message without hesitation, or unnecessary pause or stumble. I knew I was witnessing excellence and furthermore I could see from the reaction of the audience that they were equally affected.

Over the years I have seen many presentations. All presentations follow the normal distribution curve. A small percentage are excellent, a large percentage are average, and a small percentage are painful. The presentations I remember most are those that are excellent and terrible. When fortunate to witness excellence, my trust in the individual's competence is elevated. When I witness a weak presentation my trust of the individual's competence is lowered.

Being an excellent presenter is one of the greatest challenges in both business and in life. It is seldom a natural competency, but rather a developed skill. To become a great presenter follows an expected formula; preparation, practice, perform, solicit feedback and improve.

It has long been acknowledged that public speaking is the greatest fear of many individuals, it takes courage to overcome this fear. Once you step across the line and overcome fear you are now more ready to progress from competent to mastery. Presentation skill development follows the same philosophy of continuous improvement.

96

The following are practical recommendations when developing and delivering a presentation:

- **Communication Strategy:** Ask yourself these questions; "What do I want the audience to think, do or say at the end of this presentation?" Secondly, "What are the needs of the audience?" Keeping these questions in mind will keep you on track to having impactful content for your audience.
- **Preparation:** Know your information and your audience. Be mindful of the time constraints of your audience.
- **Self-awareness**: Be aware of the customer's culture and match your attire accordingly. If you are over-dressed or under-dressed the client may perceive that you have not done your research.
- **Be dynamic:** Present with energy and passion.
- **Solicit feedback:** After the presentation, ask for feedback from a colleague on what you did well and what you could improve upon. Take the feedback to heart and embrace the spirit of continuous improvement.

Achieving excellence in presentation skills is a differentiator! It will give you an advantage over the competition. It will allow you to better serve your customers and build positive perception.

Negotiation Skills

As a sales professional you will encounter many situations where you will be required to negotiate with customers. This may include negotiating price, terms and conditions and scope of work.

To satisfy your client's goals, problems and needs you follow a process where you determine solutions, estimate costs and calculate margins. In a perfect scenario, you tender an offer to your client, and they accept it without modification. However, you must be prepared for the possibility that your client may want to negotiate for a better price or terms.

The best negotiating outcomes are Win/Win. Where both you and the client feel they have a favorable deal. Although this result is desired you must be prepared for the potential outcomes of Lose/Win, Win/Lose, Lose/Lose or No Deal.

Some practical tips for negotiating include:

- **Be prepared:** The person with the most information is in a better position to achieve their desired outcome.
- **Be patient:** Do not rush a negotiation. Let the other party lead the discussion. This will provide insight into their priorities. Ask questions and clarify your understanding.
- **Be poised:** Do not become rattled by unreasonable requests. Remain calm and composed. You are best served to control your emotions.
- **Be diplomatic:** Understand your options and think in terms of "quid pro quo" that is, "something for something." What is the client will to give in exchange for their concession request?
- **Be empathic:** Try to understand the deal from the client's perspective and use language that seeks first to understand their position then to have your position understood.

- **Be fair and reasonable:** People generally view themselves as fair and reasonable. By elevating this principle into the conversation parties tend to remain open to discussion.
- **Be courageous:** You may have to walk away from the negotiation.

Customers want high quality products, speedy service and low price. Your objective is to help them get what they want. Keeping in mind that high quality products, speedy service and low price are subjective. You perform an essential role in defining objective reality. Through skillful negotiations you create the bridge for the customer to obtain the outcome they desire.

.

Sales Call Planning

Early in my sales career I attended a training class on advanced selling skills. Our Vice President of Sales was instructing us on the use of a strategic sales worksheet. It was a comprehensive document that led an individual to think about the customers goals, problems, and needs. The objective of the document was to prepare the sales colleague to handle potential client objections and reservations. It was evident that this was much more call preparation than the attendees were currently employing. One brave person asked a question to the Vice President, "This form will take quite a bit of time to complete, when do we need to use it?" the Vice President responded, "You should only use the form for the projects you want to win!" 😊

This response has resonated with me for many decades. It is as relevant today as it was then. Yet, if this concept is so logical why do so few sales reps create formal written plans for their sales calls? All major companies in this industry invest huge sums of money for sales training. One common training platform is *Acclivus R3*. This course provides the call planning forms that enable a structure for thinking. Additionally, instructors work with sales colleagues to complete the form and conduct role playing exercises to execute the call plan. All trainees can complete these exercises with relative competency by the time they complete the class.

What is surprising is that most sales colleagues do not use call planning sheets once they return from training. Some sales colleagues may use them for the first few weeks, then fall back to previous routines and habits. A small percent will embrace the logic, practice and belief that effective call planning will lead to better outcomes. Their results prove this belief to be accurate.

The essence of sales call planning is to take time to think deeply about your objectives and to develop a communication strategy. A sales call planning worksheet is a useful tool but is only as effective as the thinking that goes into its completion. You can think of sales call planning as a process. In the world of total quality management, all focus goes to improving processes which results in improved quality. The more consistent you are with your sales call planning process the better you will be at serving your clients' needs and closing orders.

All sales professionals realize that the best devised call plans do not always guarantee smooth sailing. Many unexpected issues and circumstances can affect the meeting. All one can do is prepare well and consider the curveballs that might be thrown their way. A preparation technique that has been used is role playing. This involves having a colleague or manager play the role of the client while you practice the sales call. This has been instrumental in building confidence and preparing the mind for potential objections.

Consider this; consistent application of formal sales call planning will lead to competence. Increased competence will lead to confidence. Increased confidence will lead to mastery. Increased mastery will lead to achieving greatness.

Sales Meetings

Sales meetings are a common practice in organizations that have dedicated sales personnel. They serve many purposes, but the primary functions include:

- **Communication:** A forum or the sales manager to give and receive information on the state of the business.
- **Collaboration:** A venue to share information with other sales colleagues.
- **Development:** A venue to receive training on products and/or service offerings.
- **Brainstorming:** A venue to discuss processes and improvement ideas.

Sales leaders understand that effective sales meetings can have a positive effect on organizational performance. The primary objective of the sales leader is to deliver the aggregate sales bookings required to achieve the operations revenue requirements. Achieving this goal requires accomplishing key objectives which include:

- Motivating individuals
- Creating a team culture that is energizing and cooperative
- Developing the skills and knowledge of team members
- Communicating expectations and plans
- Holding individuals accountable

The sales leader has a big challenge to effectively accomplish these objectives. They must have interactions with each sales colleague to advance each initiative. To accomplish this in a one-on-one approach becomes an impossibility as sales organizations increase in size. The leader must deploy group communications to effectively cover more ground. Thus, the importance of sales meetings.

You are a key player in this organization. You are expected to contribute professionally to the advancement of the organization's collective mission. This is to say that you are expected to demonstrate behaviors that help lead the team to greatness. Some of the behaviors that are most appreciated when it comes to sales meetings include:

- Having a positive attitude
- Bringing energy into sales meetings
- Coming prepared to contribute
- Being respectful of other's opinions
- Supporting fellow colleagues
- Following through on commitments

The sales meeting is intended to be an energizing forum for you, the other team members and the sales leader. Achieving an energizing sales meeting requires synergy. Developing synergy is tricky. It takes maturity and enlightenment on the part of a critical few. This implies the need for leadership within the ranks of sales colleagues to support the sales leader. Be that internal leader!

Mentoring

Mentoring relationships can play an important role in your development. Throughout this document I have presented the important role that others play in your development and the belief that you cannot achieve excellence without the help of others.

The objective of establishing mentoring relationships is to facilitate your development. Human development is a personal project and although organizations can facilitate training and development only the individual can realize their potential. You are accountable for your development.

In your role as a sales professional the ideal mentor is a senior sales professional. The mentor serves an important role for you in the acceleration of your development. The key aspects of the mentoring relationship include:

- A source for advice from an experienced colleague
- A resource that is readily accessible
- An individual who trustworthy and non-judgmental
- An individual who can provide coaching and feedback

The mentoring relationship is organic. It naturally develops based on the chemistry of the mentor and mentee. The relationship must be one of mutual benefit that generates energy between both parties. There is a responsibility on your part to approach the mentor with thoughtful preparation, serious participation and a commitment to act upon suggestions.

The role of the mentor is to facilitate your growth. The method and means of achieving this are expansive but one of the prudent mentoring activities is to learn from the expert.

An effective yet simple four step process is as follows:

1. The mentor does the task while the mentee watches and learns.
2. The mentor and mentee do the task together.
3. The mentee does the task while the mentor watches and gives feedback.
4. The mentee (you) does the task.

Determining the best mentor for you should be done in collaboration with your manager. Not all senior sales professionals are ideal mentors so care must be taken in the selection process. Many traits are considered when selecting a mentor, but the key criteria must be the desire to serve others.

If you are fortunate enough to be a mentee you have a responsibility to the mentor. The mentor has a full-time job, so it is essential that you respect the value of their time. Honor their support by being prepared and acting on recommendations.

As a final thought, mentoring is a continuum. At some future time, you may be called upon to be a mentor for a colleague. Learn and retain the knowledge gained from your mentoring experience. Be prepared to pay it forward.

Progress Review and Goal Setting

Enlightened organizations realize that their colleagues are their most valuable asset. Consequently, they are mindful to provide the appropriate leadership style that will best support the specific needs of each colleague. This approach is also referred to as *Situational Leadership*[11].

The practice of *Situational Leadership* starts with an understanding that individuals need various styles of leadership based on the <u>task</u> required to be completed. The manager/leader will collaborate with the colleague to determine their <u>commitment level</u> and <u>competency level</u> to effectively complete the task (Development Level). Additionally, the manager/leader must determine the leadership style that is most appropriate for the situation.

This exercise is essential in matching the colleague's development level with the leadership style. When applied correctly, the colleague makes progress in his development. The chart below depicts the four scenarios:

Development Level		Leadership Style	
D1	High Commitment Low Competency	S1	Directive
D2	Variable Commitment Some Competency	S2	Coaching
D3	Low Commitment High Competency	S3	Supportive
D4	High Commitment High Competency	S4	Delegating

With the *Situational Leadership* model there is a high level of communication and feedback on progress of the assigned task. The colleague and their manager make a bi-lateral agreement that

---

[11] Ken Blanchard, Margie Blanchard, *Situational Leadership II, 1985*

establishes the task to be accomplished, expectations and follow-up intervals to confirm expected results.

The second means of progress review occurs during regularly scheduled one-on-one meetings between you and your manager. The agenda of these one-on-one meetings is predicated on current priorities. It is typical to review your progress on major opportunities, your progress on sales activity metrics and your personal development.

On a quarterly basis you should prepare an executive summary for your manager that outlines your progress to goals. You will be best served by building your presentation into a power point deck and demonstrating your presentation skills. It is always advisable to build upon your annual business plan, analyze what is working well and what needs shoring up.

Annually you will complete a year-end assessment. These reviews are beneficial to reflect and learn about the business environment and how your aggregate commitment and competencies contributed to your results. The progress review provides guidance in establishing next year's goals.

Goals create the roadmap to success. Written goals that are reviewed regularly and shared with others have a high probability of attainment. Therefore, when done correctly, the goal setting process can be an effective and motivating exercise. Good goals follow the acronym of **SMART** which means they must be:

- **S**pecific
- **M**easurable
- **A**chievable
- **R**elevant
- **T**ime Bound

Goals need to be progressively more challenging as you grow toward greatness. It is also advisable to limit the number of goals to a critical few in the areas of financial performance, personal development and client development.

Section 6 - Account Management

Defining Account Management

As a sales colleague you are responsible for the management of an account and likely a portfolio of accounts. The term account management also implies account development which is specifically growing the annual spend of the account by offering additional products and services. One can equate that every commercial business is an account, and although this is true, not every commercial customer would be defined as a managed account. In many cases a commercial customer needs a low voltage system to serve a specific function and they do not have substantial growth potential beyond a singular project.

Large accounts are often complex. You can imagine large accounts as a campus of buildings or a singular facility with an enormous footprint. They utilize numerous systems and technologies to support their on-going operations and to protect their people and properties. Their investment in low voltage systems is substantial. They are a growing dynamic business looking for strategic relationships to improve the efficiency and security of their business operations.

Project management is not the same as account management. The Project Management Institute (PMI) defines a project as follows:

> "A temporary endeavor undertaken to create a unique product, service or result. A project is temporary in that it has a defined beginning and end in time, and therefore defined scope and resources. And a project is unique in that it is not a routine operation, but a specific set of operations designed to accomplish a singular goal."

From this definition one would deduce that an account will have numerous projects over a time period.

As account manager you can visualize several key roles:

- **Strategic partner:** Review the goals, problems and needs of the account on an on-going basis and develop recommendations as to how your organization can address these issues.
- **Relationship management:** Collect feedback on the performance of your team and facilitate process improvements. Coordinate periodic business reviews.
- **Team leader:** Act as the customer's champion and ensure the promises you made are clearly communicated to your operations team members.

As account manager you are not the project manager. The management of each project is the responsibility of the project manager. The project manager is focused on achieving and delivering a result that is on time, within budget and to the quality standard expected by the client. Within these objectives are structured activities that include the management of scope, cost, risk, procurement, resources, schedule, quality, stakeholders, changes and communications.

As account manager, it is necessary that you remain integrated with the project manager and share knowledge for the betterment of the account and project. The project manager manages the project and the sales colleague manages the account.

You, as the account manager, are the leader. You communicate a shared vision, energize your teammates and celebrate operational achievements. These leadership actions will bond you and the operations team on the journey to greatness.

Project Turnover and Kickoff Meetings

Winning the confidence of your customer and receiving an order is a euphoric feeling. Let's face it, a sales career has a distinct benefit of knowing when you have absolutely won (received an order) or when you have lost (been told the order went to the competition). Many jobs do not have the same clarity of knowing when you have absolutely won. For many sales colleagues, winning an order is the culmination of an extensive effort on very large endeavors over a long period of time. However, from the customer's perspective, the project is now in the beginning stages. Although the heavy lifting of sales activities is complete your next major function is to conduct a project turn-over meeting with your operations team and effectively kick-off the next phase of the delivery of your promise.

Think for a moment that you are a one-person company. You sold a project and now you must complete the operational aspects of engineering, product procurement, installation, commissioning and project management. You know the agreement details, there is low risk in disagreement of the scope of work. You can go about completing the operational phase with absolute confidence.

Mature organizations have learned over the years that a one-person sales/operation model is not the most efficient for growth. Today most organizations are structured with specialized assignments and job classifications which better support excellence and quality. The business model has evolved from entrepreneurial to team approach.

One of the well-known weaknesses of the team model is the inaccurate and incomplete transfer of information. These transfers are likened to the passing of a baton in a relay race. When the team has an effective hand-off, the team is better positioned to win. If the baton is dropped there is panic and less than acceptable results. This analogy correlates to the sales colleague handing off the baton (i.e. critical project information) to the operations team member.

It is safe to say that many sales representatives have dropped batons during this transfer. This has happened so often that companies have developed project turnover policies and procedures. The rationale follows the thinking of total quality management and continuous improvement. With a focus on process control, document control, knowledge transfer and planning, the likelihood of a successful project is enhanced.

Following the guidelines for project turnover is an essential responsibility of the sales colleague. But the enlightened sales professional recognizes that they can do more to affect project success through their effective leadership. Many sales reps are accused of throwing the order over the wall to operations. Other colorful descriptors like "dump and run" create a perception that sales colleagues "wash their hands" of further involvement once the order is received. To truly achieve sales greatness, you are encouraged to be the leader and champion for the customer.

As a sales professional you are a highly trained and skilled communicator. Use your communication skills to motivate your operations team. You have the opportunity and ability to create excitement about the project and to encourage achieving project greatness.

It is important to remember that throughout the sales process you and your client have developed a relationship of trust. You have made an implied promise that the organization will deliver on your commitments. The operations team is your resource to deliver upon your promise. You have much credibility to lose if things go poorly and much to gain if things go great. It is in your best interest to accept the leadership challenge and conduct effective and energizing turnover meetings.

Supporting Operations

The underlying assumption I have made with many of the topics covered in this document is that you are committed to achieve personal greatness. It is my hope that you believe that you can achieve incredible results through your attitude, effort and continuous improvement. When joining an organization, you need the help of others to learn the organizational culture, policy, procedures, mission and strategies. As you develop within the organization you become less dependent on others while you become more independent in your core responsibilities. I think you will agree that we need to be helped by others in some aspects of our work while we need to help others in different aspects. I quote the famous author, Napoleon Hill, where he states, "A human cannot exceed mediocrity without the help of others."[12]

This leads to the discussion of your role in supporting the operations department personnel. For this discussion, operations personnel would include anyone who is delivering upon your promise to the customer; operations and service managers, project managers, service technicians, installers, programmers, administrators and subcontractors. Understanding that you play a critical role as part of the project team is an important distinction from a common misconception that you sell stuff and operations takes care of stuff. I have seen the erosion of many relationships between sales teams and operations teams due to the absence of shared vision, unity and personal leadership.

---

[12] Napoleon Hill, *The Law of Success*, pp. *xxi* (*The Penguin Group, New York, 1928*)

To better exemplify, consider the roles and goals you have in supporting operations:

- **Sales Professional:** Creating high quality proposals, building a trust relationship with the client and following established guidelines for project risk reviews.
- **Communicator:** Effectively unifies all project stakeholders to a shared vision of the project, clarifies scope of work and organizes information in a logical manner.
- **Account Manager:** Vocal champion for the client, balances reasonableness, fairness and long-term objectives.
- **Motivator:** Keeps the operational team members positive, energized and focused on the mission.
- **Team Leader:** Thinks broadly and cares about the needs of others.

The roles listed above are essential. Initially not all sales colleagues perform these roles with excellence but in time their competency in these roles progressively improve. There is a myriad of variables that determine your success in these roles, the most important being the personalities of your operational team members. This is not a revelation, but instead an encouragement for the astute sales colleague to use an effective communication style to facilitate team success.

Supporting operations can be viewed as one of the most enjoyable parts of the sales colleague's assignment. Your role is to help the operational team understand the purpose and meaning of their work. When you perform this role well you build up the team's pride and self-esteem. Humans want to be part of a team and they want to make significant contributions. But far too often we see organizations lose zest and perspective regarding their critical purpose. It requires leadership at all levels to achieve extraordinary outcomes. You can be the catalyst to create extraordinary outcomes. I encourage you to support your operations team members enthusiastically. The benefits will far exceed your expectations.

Key Account Management Process

In a previous section I described the difference between account management and project management. In this section I want to discuss the process of managing large accounts. The terms key accounts, major accounts and large accounts are all synonymous for the purpose of this discussion. By any name, the accounts described are the Big Rocks of your business plan. The Big Rocks analogy follows the 80/20 principle in that 80% of the financial results come from 20% of your customers. With this understanding it is clear to see the impact and importance of your large accounts.

Large account management is complex. For most sales colleagues it is not intuitive nor easy. But the good news is that there is extensive information and training programs that lead the motivated individual through the discovery process. One well known program has been developed by The Miller Heiman Company titled the Large Account Management Process (LAMP)[13]. It is suggested reading for individuals looking for mastery.

The basic premise of LAMP is this; in order to achieve long-term profitable relationships with your key customers, you must make consistent, measurable contributions to their profitability and their customer relationships. You must make contributions to your key accounts that ensure their success. This is very different than normal sales transactions where parties are focused ideally on a win/win contract for a needed service. With LAMP you are playing the long game with the understanding that by shifting your emphasis to the care and best interests of your client you will be rewarded at the appropriate time.

The first step of the Large Account Management Process (LAMP) is selecting customers that would benefit from your commitment and where the organization can add value to their business operations.

---

[13] Robert B. Miller, Stephen E. Heiman, *The New Successful Large Account Management, (Business Plus, New York, 2005)*

Not all customers share a philosophy of partnership. Many have a corporate culture where they want to keep a competitive climate between vendors. They prioritize cost management over the value of relationship.

The second step is to assess how your organization is perceived by the account. This is a multi-layered evaluation of your organization as well as the perception of you and each team member that works on the account. Additionally, it considers the perceptions of each stakeholder, decision maker, sponsor and influencer. To assess these considerations the LAMP process requires much analysis by you, management and operations personnel.

The next step is to build your strategic plan that is qualitative. How will you demonstrate added quality to the benefit of the client? Your goal is to build positive perception within your client's organization and to move up the buy-sell hierarchy. The graphic depicted below illustrates the five levels of the buy-sell hierarchy and you should be able to determine where you stand with your large accounts. As you build your strategy, you should share your plan with the client. They will guide you to success as it is in their best interest. If they are unwilling to provide meaningful input, this may signal that they are not a good candidate for LAMP.

Remember the following key points:

- Large Account Management requires significant effort, but the rewards will follow.
- LAMP will require significant mental energy in strategic planning.
- Not all customers are good candidates for LAMP.
- Large Account Management is not a one-person show. It takes a team. You are the leader.

LAMP is not easily mastered. It is a journey of self-discovery and client discovery. I encourage you to read the LAMP book and completing the templates.

Large Account Management
Buy-Sell Hierarchy

Make an Important Contribution

Decrease

Competition

Price Sensitivity

Features Importance

Increase

Contribute to Organizational Issues — 5

Contribute to Business Issues — 4

Provide "Good" Service and Support — 3

Deliver "Good" Products and/or Service — 2

Deliver Commodity that Meets Specification — 1

Sell Product

Service then Reward

Sales professionals understand that they must deliver results. They understand they play an essential role in maintaining the health of the business. Their objective is to close enough business to build backlog as a source of future revenue. To achieve this outcome, they must focus on inputs; identifying opportunities, qualifying leads, presenting solutions, building proposals, and resolving concerns.

To be rewarded with sales orders (bookings) the sales professional must provide service in equal or greater value. This is the natural law of cause and effect. Earl Nightingale discusses this proven principle in his *Lead the Field* program where he details how our rewards in life will always match our service.[14] Every culture has a proverb that acknowledges this principle, one common saying "As ye sow, so shall ye reap" speaks to the action-reaction effect.

Many sales colleagues can become frustrated when they lose an order. Most colleagues will diagnose reason for loss as <u>low price by competitor</u>. In contrast when an order is won the sales colleague will typically cite <u>superior relationship with client</u>. A win versus a loss are not perceived with objectivity. More accurately, the win or loss is a direct relation to the level of service provided.

If you are not happy with your rewards you must examine your service. It is common and logical to mimic the strategies and tactics of the top performers. These peak performers have developed skills, knowledge, habits and relationships that enabled them to provide a superior service, and consequently, receive superior reward. Learn from the best but also understand that if you want to surpass the best you must find ways to increase your service more than your predecessors.

---

[14] Earl Nightingale, *Lead the Field, audio program, (Nightingale-Conant, Chicago,1990)*

Think of creative ways to increase your service. How you can shape a client's perception of you as the following:

- Indispensable business partner
- Trusted consultant
- Go-To professional

As we presented in the LAMP process, think about adding value to the client relationship. Focus on helping your customers help their customers. Discovering the solutions that will increase your value and consequently your rewards.

Partnership Development

The desire of the organization is to build long term partnerships with all accounts. Most accounts do not resemble deep committed partnerships for many reasons. One reason may be that the client has engaged your business for a project need and does not see the benefit of an on-going service relationship. A second reason may be that their core philosophy is that they prefer to transact with an approved vendor list and attempt to keep all competitors on an equal playing field.

Fortunately, many key accounts have a substantial investment in low voltage systems. Furthermore, they understand the importance to their on-going performance as a component of their operations and risk mitigation. These accounts have goals, problems and needs that you and your organization have the ability address and solve. But you must also understand that your clients have options on who they select to handle their needs.

In our earlier discussion on the Buy-Sell Hierarchy we identified five levels of relationship with large accounts. Level 5 is where we operate as a business partner. Trust exists between you and your points of contact as well as at the organizational level. If the relationship is below level 5 you have work ahead of you. You will need to determine how you can increase your perceived value through providing greater service.

Moving up the Buy-Sell Hierarchy can be an uncertain process. It can be affected by the following:

- Personalities of stakeholders
- Business philosophy of the client
- Strength of your operations
- Strength of competitors
- Your power as a sales professional

Ultimately, you and your leadership team will need to assess and determine if we can attain partnership footing with the account. The mechanics of achieving level 5 partnership is detailed in the LAMP process. This requires team engagement, strategic thinking and a desire on the part of the client.

Achieving level 5 partnership is challenging and once accomplished the celebration is short lived. To maintain this status requires consistent excellent performance by you and the operations. But like most things in life, we are either growing or dying. Status quo is not acceptable long term. You must continue to add greater value by increasing your service.

The starting point for the continuous improvement approach must start with diagnosing how current performance is valued by the account. This can only be accomplished through communications with the client. The means of doing this is typically through the following approaches:

- Quality Review Meeting
- Quarterly Business Review Meeting
- Voice of the Customer Meeting

Regardless of the title of the meeting, the objective is as follows:

- Create an agreed upon agenda
- Listen and learn from the stakeholders
- Memorialize the meeting through formal notes
- Develop action plans
- Follow through with implementation

The frequency of partnership development meetings will vary by client but generally meeting on a quarterly basis is most common.

Synergy

The term <u>Account Manager</u> defines a position and a responsibility. The term <u>Account Management</u> defines a function and a process. Managing key accounts requires a team effort. Achieving total customer satisfaction requires a team of individuals with specific attributes that include:

- Commitment to excellence
- Proactive communication
- Technical proficiency
- Energized attitude

Above all the team must deliver results and make significant contributions to the client's profitability.

Achieving this vision is complex and allusive. Even with a team of talented individuals that have the skills, knowledge and desire there is no guarantee that the cumulative result is greatness in the eyes of the client. To increase the probability of success you need to synergize the team. Synergy is defined as the cooperation of two or more individual agents to produce a combined effect greater than the sum of the individual parts. Stated another way, synergy is when one plus one equals more than two.

Synergy can be found in high performing teams. Think of personal examples of when you were part of a team that accomplished extraordinary results. Team greatness was achieved through the combination of diverse individual talents working in harmony for a common goal.

Napoleon Hill, author of the book *The Law of Success*[15] developed a principle he coined as the "Mastermind Alliance." The basic tenants of the Mastermind Alliance are that it consists of two or more minds

---

[15] Napoleon Hill, *The Law of Success, pp. xxi (The Penguin Group, New York, 1928)*

working actively together in perfect harmony toward a common definite objective. Through a mastermind alliance you can appropriate and use the full strength of the experience, training and knowledge of others just as if they were your own. As you interpret these thoughts, you see your team as your Mastermind Alliance. You have a shared vision, you have the vast experience, training and knowledge of your fellow colleagues, now you need to synergize.

Leadership ignites the spark of synergy. You as the Account Manager can create the extraordinary through your leadership. There are no absolutes when it comes to leadership style and approach, but a positive attitude is critical. In 1948 a study was conducted about the principles of leadership; here are some of the relevant findings[16]:

- Know yourself and seek self-improvement
- Be technically proficient
- Seek responsibility and take responsibility for your actions
- Set the example
- Look out for the welfare of your team
- Keep your team informed
- Develop a sense of responsibility among your team
- Make sound and timely decisions

The secrets of success are not secret. Achieving success in account management starts with you, the account manager. You can achieve greatness every day through your individual efforts, but you cannot achieve team greatness without synergy with others. You are the catalyst!

---

[16] Ed Ruggero, Dennis F. Haley, *The Leader's Compass, (Academy Leadership, King of Prussia, PA, 2005)*

Section 7 - Achieve Personal Greatness

Personal Leadership

The world at large has a fascination with leadership. You can find evidence of this at a library, bookstore or internet search on the topic. Moreover, we can see examples of the presence or absence of leadership in the daily news feeds. In our business lives we define leadership as the influencing of people by providing purpose, direction and motivation while operating to accomplish the goals and improving the organization. It would be logical to conclude that highly successful organizations have highly effective leadership.

What about your organization, the business of **YOU**? You are the leader of your life and consequently provide personal leadership. Personal Leadership is the ability to define a direction for your leadership and life, and to move in that direction with consistency and clarity.

Defining the direction in your life begins with understanding your life's mission. The process of defining your mission answers the key questions of:

- What do you want to be?
- What do you want to achieve?
- What principles do you want to possess and live by?

This exercise is wholistic and addresses the various roles and goals of your life, not just your business goals. This is not an easy task and surprisingly few people endeavor to wrestle with this soul-searching exercise. Those that do, find greater clarity of purpose, life balance and energy.

Defining and guiding your life's mission is personal. Only you know what is right for you. It starts with your spirit, your inner voice that guides you to the things that matter most to you. In his book *The 8th Habit* [17], Steven Covey provides a model of how he defines and guides

---

[17] Steven R. Covey, *The 8th Habit*, (Simon & Schuster, New York, 2004)

personal mission. The better you become at expanding these human capacities the greater your life becomes:

- **Conscience:** The guiding force to vision, discipline and passion.
- **Vision:** Seeing with the mind's eye the possibilities in your life.
- **Discipline:** Paying the price to bring that vision into reality.
- **Passion:** The strength in conviction that sustains the discipline to achieve the vision.

Personal leadership is a continuous journey. As your personal leadership develops, your vision of your life's possibilities expands. As you enjoy victories in life, your discipline is further strengthened, and your passion grows. As your passion grows, you enjoy greater victories, see greater possibilities and your vision evolves.

You are the hero of your life story. Will it be an epic victory or a tragic ending? The story will be determined by your personal leadership. The template for *The Hero's Journey* developed by Joseph Campbell[18] depicts the cycle of most adventure stories. You are called to adventure. You will face challenges and temptations. By developing your personal leadership, you will be prepared to overcome life's obstacles and continue to grow to greatness.

---

[18] Joseph Campbell, *A Hero's Journey, The Hero with a Thousand Faces, 1949*

Adversity

On this marathon of life and on your quest to achieve greatness I can promise you that you will face adversity. In the previous section I presented the model of *The Hero's Journey* where the hero crosses the threshold to their call to adventure and to face challenges and temptations, otherwise known as adversity. Every hero's story has adversity, and certainly the greater the adversity the greater the story, if it ends in victory.

In this section I want to provide some perspectives on adversity. The first perspective is that adversity is an opportunity for growth. We live our daily lives in one of three zones; comfort zone, discomfort zone or panic zone. <u>We learn best in the discomfort zone</u>. The philosopher Epictetus stated that every difficulty in life presents us with an opportunity to turn inward and to invoke our own submerged inner resources. Stated another way, utilize your problem-solving skills. As you develop your creative thinking and effectively solve problems you become consciously competent. This developed skill stimulates your transformation to next level greatness.

The second perspective is that we need adversity to keep life exciting. If life is always operating in the comfort zone you will tend to become complacent. Complacency does not bring joy to life but excellence does. The philosopher Seneca offers two thoughts which are excellence withers without adversity and secondly, no person is more unhappy than he who never faces adversity, for he is not permitted to prove himself.

The third perspective is to embrace adversity as a gift. Cory Booker, the Mayor of Newark, N.J. was quoted as saying "What more could one ask for in life than to be given an impossible challenge." In your role it will be unlikely that you will be given an impossible challenge, but you will encounter big challenges. Look for and embrace the difficult assignments. They will accelerate your growth.

Let me give you a few examples of adversity that have presented themselves in our industry:

- **Loss of confidence:** If you are new to the industry you may feel you are inferior and question if you have made the right career decision.
- **Embarrassment:** You may be put into situations where you cannot demonstrate competency for a situation. You fear making mistakes.
- **Insecurity:** You internally question if you are providing enough value. You worry about how your manager perceives your progress.
- **Underperformance to goals:** You may have times when you are not achieving performance goals or activity goals.
- **Stress:** You may be putting excessive pressure on yourself.
- **Fatigue:** You are burning the candle at both ends. You are working long days and weekends and not getting enough sleep, down-time, exercise or nutrition.
- **Difficult teammates:** You encounter colleagues who are challenging and make work more difficult than necessary. They do not respect core values.
- **Unprofessional clients:** You encounter customers that lack civility, integrity or display arrogance and ego.
- **Family pressures:** You have personal demands that require attention and these conflict with business commitments.
- **Confusion:** You may feel overwhelmed and revert to a mental gridlock.
- **Duplicitous dealings:** When you are being lied to or disparaged without understanding the motive.
- **Superior competitor:** You may feel your rival has an advantage in some respects.
- **Downturn in the economy:** Market dynamics may reduce the number of opportunities or slow client spending.
- **Subcontractor gifts:** A subcontractor may entice you personally with monetary and non-monetary gifts in exchange for business.

- **Bribery:** There may be public officials or industry participants who suggest enticements in order to expedite work.
- **Collusion:** A competitor suggests a form of bid rigging or price fixing.
- **Mistakes:** You may make mistakes which cost the company financial loss and or negatively affect its reputation.

This partial list makes clear that adversity is to be expected. Take heart to know that all sales professionals have encountered many of these challenges. They are hurdles that must be cleared. You are expected to handle adversity with calm confidence. You have the strength and personal resources to handle most challenges. When you are not enough, know that you have the support of your manager and colleagues to guide you through these challenges. You must overcome your adversity; you are on a Hero's Journey.

Mastery

Achieving personal greatness in your role as a sales professional is no easy task. To become an elite performer in any profession takes extraordinary effort over a prolonged period. Malcolm Gladwell, author of the book *Tipping Point*[19] speaks to the topic of outliers, those individuals who have accomplished a rare level of excellence. He provides an example of the Beatles and their meteoric rise to fame in America. What few people know is that in their early teen years they began performing at a Hamburg, Germany club where they performed 7 days a week for 8-hour sets and did this for months at a time. It was determined that they had performed over 10,000 hours prior to their American introduction.

Through his research, Gladwell determined that the 10,000-hour rule held true in many examples and supports his conclusion that there are very few overnight success stories but rather effort brings rewards in direct proportion.

Mastery must be achieved over time. 10,000 hours of effort is a good milestone, but it might take more based on these factors:

- The quality of effort.
- Your collaboration with peers.
- The mentoring and coaching from leaders.
- Your development of industry knowledge, strategic thinking and critical thinking skills.

Your journey to mastery is best served with a map. The map starts with assessing your current location and then plotting a course to lead you to the desired location (greatness). You are best served to confront reality and make periodic adjustments to stay on course. This is the essence of setting goals on a regular basis and conducting

---

[19] Malcolm Gladwell, *The Tipping Point: How Little Things Make a Big Difference*, (Little, Brown, 2000)

annual assessments of your performance. Your focus must be on continuous improvement.

Experience by itself does not guarantee success. However, experience with insight and assimilation will accelerate your journey to the promised land. The more sales repetitions you make, the more experience you are acquiring. Repetitions build strength and competency. Increased competency leads to confidence. Increased confidence leads to mastery.

There is nothing simple about achieving mastery as a sales professional in the low voltage industry. Very few sales colleagues achieve this level. Many sales professionals improve and become highly competent and consistent performers. They make a good living and contribute meaningfully to organizational success. There is a heavy price to pay to achieve mastery and personal greatness. I encourage you to take the journey, pay your dues, get better every day and achieve greatness!

Success Model

Mastery is achieving personal success at the highest level. It is independence. Beyond mastery and independence is the concept of interdependence. It aligns with our discussion on synergy. As you continue to grow personally and professionally you will achieve individual greatness. But for the organization to achieve greatness it takes more; it takes an army of talented and committed colleagues. The purpose of this section is to discuss a success model that intends to simplify how organizations achieve their vision and mission.

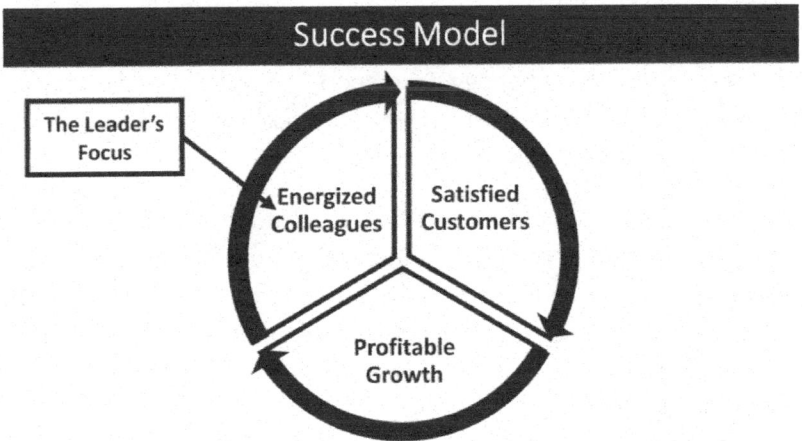

The success model recognizes three elements of a continuum, energized colleagues, satisfied customers and profitable growth. Thinking through this mental model one can see that there is a logical starting point on this continuum, it starts with energized colleagues. As the diagram shows, the leader's focus is on creating energized colleagues.

Picture an organization where all colleagues are energized about their personal mission, where they have clarity of vision. They understand their role within the bigger picture. They feel respected, valued and loved. They have a belief that they are here to serve the

133

client's needs. They are best prepared to solve the client's business, technical and emotional needs. When we create an army of energized colleagues it becomes the input that transforms the customer experience into one of satisfaction.

Once the output of customer satisfaction is achieved, the input for profitable growth is possible. The inputs to profitable growth include:

- Timely payment of invoices
- Additional project work
- Service contract work
- Expansion of other low voltage system work
- Favorable references for other clients
- A customer for life

In addition to the benefits that come directly from the customer, another amazing thing happens, our energized colleagues gain higher levels of self-esteem as they recognize the excellence of their work. This builds competence and confidence.

In this last stage, the output of profitable growth now becomes the input for energized colleagues. Because of profitable growth the organization now needs more energized colleagues. The organization now needs to promote from within to expand the culture through mentoring and coaching. The success model continues to expand as the culture of energized colleagues expands.

Here is where you fit into the equation. Within the box that shows The Leader's Focus write your name. This implies that you are the leader, and you are. Your focus is twofold; first, demonstrate your personal leadership and be an energized colleague. Secondly, be the internal leader that supports and enables teammates to achieve their objectives. This is the essence of personal leadership. You have the power to transform your world, the world of your fellow colleagues and that of your customers.

Sustained Energy

When you turn on a light switch you are connecting a circuit that provides electrical energy to the lightbulb. That connected power causes illumination of light in the area. How does the human body activate energy? Without getting into quantum physics we have a basic understanding that our cells are likened to mini power plants that create energy from the fuels we provide in the form of food, water, air, sunlight, movement, sleep and thoughts.

Energy is the power required to do virtually everything. With optimal energy we are powerful! Our mental and physical capacities are working in lockstep. When our energy levels are low or depleted, we feel lethargic, our desire to work is compromised. It stands to reason that in order to serve the world and to accomplish our life's mission we must have energy.

The benefit of having energy may be better described by its inverse, that is, "Fatigue makes cowards of us all." You have meaningful work that needs to be accomplished and being fatigued impairs your ability to achieve your cause. Sustained energy is an absolute benefit and a strategic advantage.

There is abundant information on how the various fuels work to create energy, it's my intention to provide functional recommendations for you to consider that will unquestionably increase your energy levels:

- **Food:** Do not eat junk! Rather fuel yourself with nutrient rich foods from nature. Vegetables and fruits. Eat organic. Eliminate refined sugars.
- **Water:** Essential for our body functions. Water is essential in detoxifying our body. The quality of your water supply matters.
- **Breathing**: Focused breathing techniques will increase oxygenation which will support mental and physical functionality. (search Wim Hoff on YouTube).

135

- **Sunlight:** The sun provides vitamin D and is an essential source of life energy.
- **Exercise:** Our cells respond to exercise by repairing and strengthening muscles and body functions. Stress your body through regular exercise.
- **Sleep:** Your body needs time to recover and rejuvenate. Your brain must process the day's events.
- **Thought:** You become what you think about. Energy follows thought.

The expression "It's simple but it's not easy" applies to this list of recommendations. In your quest to achieve greatness you will make regular sacrifices. You will give up sleep to maximize work hours, you may eat on the run and consume convenience foods, you may skip exercising because of the fatigue of long days. I encourage you to be mindful that you have the power to increase your power. With self-awareness and education, you can make these fuel sources a catalyst for increasing and sustaining energy. On the flip side, abuse or inattention to these fuels can lead to fatigue, and consequently, sub-optimal performance.

Self-Awareness

Many years ago, I heard the quote, "We measure others by their actions, we measure ourselves by our intentions." As I reflected on this statement, it struck me just how logical and obvious this concept is.

At the heart of this quote is how each of us interpret our world, our awareness of others and our awareness of ourselves. I am inclined to believe that most people think of themselves in a positive light, because they believe their intentions are good. I would say the same about myself. I have had numerous situations where others have interpreted my actions as conflicting with my intentions. Conversely, I have had experiences where I saw the actions of others not reflecting their true intentions.

What does this discussion have to do with achieving personal greatness as a sales professional? Self-awareness is a trait that guides you to be honest <u>with</u> yourself <u>about</u> yourself. You can evaluate the opening quote and realize that others are evaluating your every action, which is where the expression "perception is reality" has its foundation. From the way you greet others, the topics you discuss, your organization, your preparedness, your attire, and your energy level all form perception. Everything counts.

Understanding self-awareness also helps you in relating with clients, colleagues and other stakeholders. You are wired to measure others by their actions. With your self-awareness you can search for greater insight, to seek to understand how actions and intentions of others align. What I am describing is a great power, the freedom you possess to choose your response to any given situation. Victor Frankl explains this revelation in his book *Man's Search for Meaning* [20]. Frankl was a prison of war in World War II, although he was treated inhumanly, stripped of his dignity and had all of his rights removed, he realized no one could take away his last freedom, his freedom to choose his

---

[20] Victor Frankl, *Man's Search for Meaning, (Beacon Press, 1959)*

response to his situation. His revelation was that in the gap between a stimulus and a response we have a freedom. The freedom to choose a response.

Rather than reacting to the initial interpretation of another person's actions, instead use your self-awareness and seek to understand. Give the benefit of doubt that the intentions of others are positive. Choose a response that leads to positive results.

Self-awareness is not a panacea to every challenging situation, but it is a necessary guide to make you honestly assess situations, to learn and grow from each interaction. Observe the excellence in others and model those behaviors that support your vision. At the same time, notice behaviors that are counterproductive in yourself and build your personal development plan. Transform your weakness into strength. Your intention is to achieve personal greatness. Are your actions aligned with your intentions?

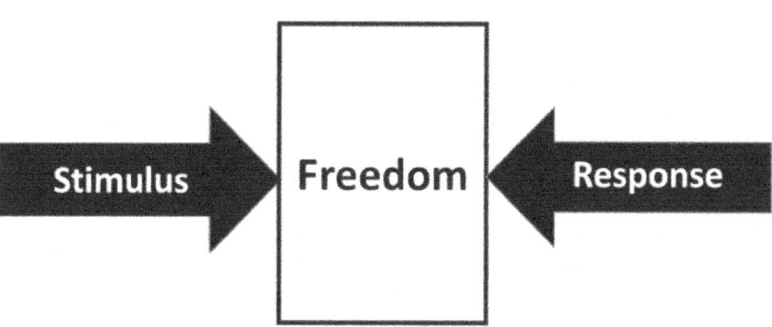

Self-Actualization

In his book *The Seven Habits of Highly Effective People* Steven Covey presents the concept of developing your life's mission. Covey's Habit #2, <u>Begin with the End in Mind</u> [21] encourages the reader to think about their own funeral and to visualize how family members and friends describe the positive impact you had on their lives. By thinking in these terms one can be challenged to ask the important questions about life and its meaning.

What do you want out of your earthly experience? What brings you the feelings of contentment, pride, joy, happiness and peace? Many have taken a psychology course and were instructed on humanistic psychological theory. In this course the central subject is the hierarchy of needs and the concept of <u>self-actualization</u> as defined by Abraham Maslow[22]. As the model depicts, individuals must continually satisfy each lower level need on the hierarchy in linear progression. According to Maslow, the highest level of human need is self-actualization which represents the growth of an individual toward the fulfillment of their life's mission.

This is heady stuff, but think about your life's journey, your mission, and where you currently sit on the hierarchy:

- **Physiological:** Are your level 1 needs met? Do you have enough food and water?
- **Safety:** Safety needs include a place to live and security from physical harm. Do you feel this need is met?
- **Love and Belonging:** Do you belong to a family or groups within the community where you feel love and acceptance?

---

[21] Steven R. Covey, *The 7 Habits of Highly Effective People, pp. 102-153 (Simon & Schuster, New York, 2004)*
[22] Abraham Maslow, *A Theory of Human Motivation (Psychological Review, 1943)*

- **Esteem:** Level 4 asks if your self-esteem is satisfied. Do you feel like you are contributing to society and you are respected and appreciated?
- **Self-Actualization:** Do you sense that you have fulfilled your potential for inner growth? Do you see the value you bring the world? Have you achieved integrity of being the best version of yourself?

Maslow's Hierarchy of Needs

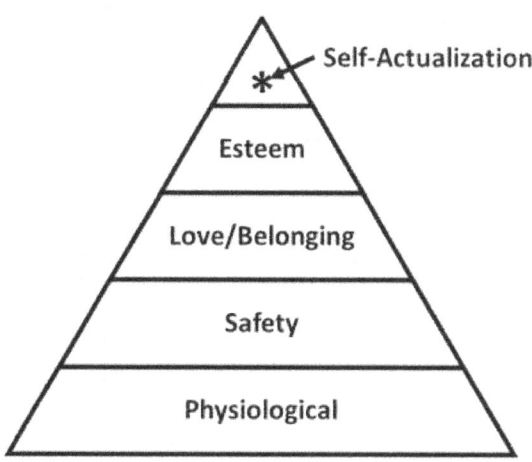

As a sales professional the world is your oyster. You have the opportunity within the low voltage industry to serve the marketplace by:

- Helping customers satisfy their goals, problems and needs.
- Providing a level of service excellence that has never been experienced before.
- Producing results that are superior by any standard.

As you imagine your progression toward personal greatness you can see how you move fluidly through the lower levels. The reality check often comes to sales colleagues in achieving and maintaining their esteem. Selling is demanding and competitive. You will face many disappointments, there may be periods when you are not meeting expectations and will feel that you have lost the esteem of others. Persist! Have grit! Once you have climbed your mountain and achieved mastery you control your self-esteem.

Self-Actualization is your final summit! Much like Everest, many attempt it, but few achieve it. Think of Self-Esteem as your final basecamp, you can now master your Everest quest and accomplish your life's mission. You will be challenged, you will fatigue, you will question whether the mission is worthy of the effort. You know you must persist. It is at those moments that greatness presents itself and breakthrough occurs. You have realized your potential.

Achieve Personal Greatness

Our society is enamored with award celebrations, we see them televised for the Grammys, the Oscars, the Tonys and the ESPYs. Most companies have excellence awards where they celebrate the "Best Of" performances in many categories. These can be a strong motivator for individuals. To win the esteem of colleagues that are respected has a lasting impression.

The one downside to "Best Of" awards is that they are often subjective. Think about figure skating or a slam dunk contest, the winners are selected by a panel of judges who may differ in their scoring criteria. Objective awards, based on absolute numbers, pose their own unique challenge. Each sales colleague is dealt a unique hand: territory, customer base, company reputation, competition and local economy. The deck may be stacked in favor or against. The other downside of the "Best Of" award culture is that there is only one winner. We accept and celebrate this approach, however there is something greater to be considered, <u>achieving personal greatness.</u>

In my first managerial assignment I was scheduling a year-end review meeting with the local team and felt inclined to provide "Best Of" awards to top performers in sales, service and administration. When I took an honest and objective look at the results, I realized that the awards did little to further motivate the winners and even less to motivate those who did not win. Not to suggest that others could not win in the future, but it struck me that if the intent was to motivate the <u>group</u>, the "Best Of" approach was of limited benefit.

I first experienced the concept of <u>achieving personal greatness</u> from reading John Wooden's book titled *Wooden on Leadership*[23]. In his book he details his philosophy of achieving success with his graphic representation of a pyramid containing the key elements that an individual must master on their journey to success. His definition of

---

[23] John Wooden, Steve Jamison, *Wooden on Leadership, (McGraw Hill, New York, 2005)*

success was to <u>achieve personal greatness</u>. The idea of achieving personal greatness has resonated with me since that day and remains a cornerstone of this guide.

The beauty of chasing personal greatness is that it is not mutually exclusive. For me to win, you do not need to lose. We all can win the award for achieving personal greatness. The challenge with employing the "Best Of" awards is that not all playing fields are level. When pursuing personal greatness, it does not matter if the playing field is level, you willingly accept the situation at hand, and you utilize the knowledge, skills, energy and determination to become the best version of yourself. It is also important to forewarn that achieving personal greatness cannot be realized by setting soft goals. You must be willing to stretch yourself. You must be willing to make personal sacrifice and push yourself mentally and physically on a regular basis. This is where you need both clear and objective self-awareness as well as feedback from others that you trust.

I wish you great fortune and much success on your journey to achieve personal greatness. I trust that you will encounter extreme challenges and that you have the fortitude to attack them head-on. With every victory you will grow stronger and more confident. The life of the sales professional is not easy, and be thankful that it is not, for the joy is in the struggle. Win the battles and achieve personal greatness.

About Bernot Best

The mission of Bernot Best is to lead, serve and teach organizations and their key colleagues who are engaged in the low voltage industry.

Bernot Best was founded with the vision of helping clients be the best they can be. We focus on developing personal leadership, business acumen, strategic planning and management skills. We approach this through creating customized transformation plans that define key development objectives, collaborate on a desired end state and build a program map to deliver the result.

Andy Bernot is the President of Bernot Best. He began his sales career in the low voltage industry in 1982. He has held leadership positions for the past 30 years.

For information on how Bernot Best can support your quest to achieve personal greatness, team greatness or organizational greatness you can contact us via email at andy@bernotbest.com

References

1) Kenneth Blanchard, Ph.D., Spencer Johnson, M.D., *The One-Minute Sales Person*
2) David Mayer, Herbert Greenberg, *What Makes a Good Salesman (Harvard Business Review July-August 2006)*
3) Steven R. Covey, *The 7 Habits of Highly Effective People, pp.73-101 (Simon & Schuster, New York, 2004)*
4) National Training Laboratories, *Bethel, Maine*
5) Napoleon Hill, *The Law of Success, pp. xxi (The Penguin Group, New York, 1928)*
6) Steven R. Covey, *The 7 Habits of Highly Effective People, pp.154-193 (Simon & Schuster, New York, 2004)*
7) Steven R. Covey, *The 7 Habits of Highly Effective People, pp.154-193 (Simon & Schuster, New York, 2004)*
8) Tony Alessandra, Phil Wexler, Rick Barrera, *Non-Manipulative Selling, 1987*
9) Earl Nightingale, *The Strangest Secret, audio cd, 1986 (Nightingale-Conant, Chicago)*
10) Acclivus Corporation, *R3 Sales Excellence, 2003*
11) Ken Blanchard, Margie Blanchard, *Situational Leadership II, 1985*
12) Napoleon Hill, *The Law of Success, pp. xxi (The Penguin Group, New York, 1928)*
13) Robert B. Miller, Stephen E. Heiman, *The New Successful Large Account Management, (Business Plus, New York, 2005)*
14) Earl Nightingale, *Lead the Field, audio program, (Nightingale-Conant, Chicago,1990)*
15) Napoleon Hill, *The Law of Success, pp. xxi (The Penguin Group, New York, 1928)*
16) Ed Ruggero, Dennis F. Haley, *The Leader's Compass, (Academy Leadership, King of Prussia, PA, 2005)*
17) Steven R. Covey, *The 8th Habit, (Simon & Schuster, New York, 2004)*

18) Joseph Campbell, *The Hero's Journey, The Hero with a Thousand Faces, 1949*

19) Malcolm Gladwell, *The Tipping Point: How Little Things Make a Big Difference, (Little, Brown, 2000)*

20) Victor Frankl, *Man's Search for Meaning, (Beacon Press, 1959)*

21) Steven R. Covey, *The 7 Habits of Highly Effective People, pp. 102-153 (Simon & Schuster, New York, 2004)*

22) Abraham Maslow, *A Theory of Human Motivation (Psychological Review, 1943)*

23) John Wooden, Steve Jamison, *Wooden on Leadership, (McGraw Hill, New York, 2005)*

Bernot Best   Greatness Guide